W9-BDH-315

Permission to be BOLD

A Guide to
Loving Yourself,
Living Fully, and
Leaving Your
Mark on the
World

BARBARA VALENTINE
GUSTAVSON

Keep your dreams alive!

Barb Gel

Permission to be BOLD – A Guide to Loving Yourself,
Living Fully, and Leaving Your Mark on the World
by Barbara Valentine Gustavson
Published by LEAD EDGE PRESS

Copyright © 2018 by Barbara Gustavson

All rights reserved. This book was self-published by the author under Lead Edge Press. No part of this book may be reproduced in any form or by any electronic or mechanical means, including information storage and retrieval systems, without written permission from the author, except in the case of a reviewer, who may quote brief passages embodied in critical articles or a review.

LEAD EDGE PRESS
c/o Discover Next Step
P.O. Box 9172
Fredericksburg, Virginia 22403

Writing contributions:
Stephanie Wetzel, Freelance Editor/Writer
Chris Jones with *Chris Jones Ink*

Editors: Maude Campbell and Amy Metheny

Cover and design: Ryan Biore

Published in the United States by Lead Edge Press
ISBN: 978-0-9976872-2-4

First Edition – December 2018

http://barbaragustavson.com

Dedication

To Michael and Ryan,

Your curiosity increased my hunger for learning.

Your ideas ignited my creativity.

Your heart expanded my capacity to love.

Your courage inspired me to find my "BOLD."

Thank you for the gift of a lifetime!

Mom

Epigraph

If you want something you've never had,
you have to do something you've never done.

— John C. Maxwell

Contents

Foreword

Dear Reader, I am so glad this book found its way into your hands because from now on your life will never be the same. I know that sounds dramatic, and perhaps a little scary, but I am being honest.

Reading this book, allowing its gentle wisdom to fill your mind and settle into your heart, and giving yourself permission to be bold can change you in ways you can't imagine.

I have been working in the personal growth and development field as a psychotherapist and coach for the last 30 years. In that time, the self-help industry has exploded with books, seminars, and workshops promising to deliver the secret recipe to getting what you want and living the perfect life. All you have to do is follow their "unique" step-by-step blueprint. But that's not how change happens. There is no one-size-fits-all, easy-peasy five-step system for self-mastery that creates immediate happiness and fulfillment.

Powerful change that lasts starts with giving yourself permission to love who you are (the good, the bad, and the ugly), to live fully (without apology), and to leave your mark on the world. This amazing adventure will be filled with trial and error, successes and failures, missteps and perfect landings, baby steps and big leaps…and everything in between.

Barbara is the perfect truth guide to help you no matter where you are on your path. Her wisdom and compassion come from her own incredible journey in which she has overcome insurmountable obstacles, embraced the "broken" parts of herself, found her voice, and committed to making the world a better place. Barbara is one of the most thoughtful, compassionate, kind, and brave women I know. Those lucky enough to know her are better for it. Since you have chosen this book (or perhaps it chose you), you will get to know Barbara, too.

Through her story and the stories she shares about others, you will understand how the decision to be bold in big and small ways every single day empowers you to be an active participant and powerful creator of your life instead of a passive bystander waiting to see what happens. In a time where opinions are divided and fear and mistrust weigh heavily on our hearts, encouraging us to shrink down and play it safe, Barbara's call to be bold is a light shining in the darkness. I'm glad you answered her call and are joining the tribe of brave souls ready for change. The world is waiting for you.

Enjoy the journey!

— Melanie Yost, LCSW
Personal Development Coach,
B.S. Slayer,
Author of *Give from the Heart,
Receive What You Are Worth*
www.melanieyost.com

Chapter 1
Step Boldly

It's better to step boldly, cross the line, and suffer the consequences than to stare at the line the rest of your life.

— Unknown

D o you remember the game "Mother May I?" In this classic game of imagination played with friends, one person is picked as the "mother" leader and they stand on the other side of everyone else. Each player has to seek the leader's permission to advance forward by asking questions. The object of the game is to get enough permissions to be the first one to cross the playing field and tag the "mother" leader. When you do, you become the new leader and the game restarts.

As a young girl, I loved this game! We would ask things like, "Mother, may I sit down?" or "Mother, may I take three giant steps?" If whoever was the leader said "yes," you got permission to advance forward and ask another question. If the person said "no," you couldn't move. You would have to wait until your next turn.

While it may sound like a silly child's game, "Mother May I?" has become a real-life commentary on our human behavior. Consider how often you've wanted to change your career or job, or try out a new idea, hobby, or strategy, only to ask for or wait for someone else's permission or encouragement to pursue it first.

When you think about it, many of us have been playing "Mother May I?" all our life, we just didn't know it. We often do things with hesitation and reservation. We have a habit of silently waiting for others to give us permission to live our lives.

What's the Big Deal About Permission?

This book you hold in your hands unveils a powerful tool that can help unlock purpose, happiness, and whatever success means to you. It's a tool that has had a profound impact on me, and I believe it can have the same impact on you. This is a tool you can't simply just read about and voila! You're there. You have to learn to pick it up and use it for yourself in order to discover its power. You have to put down the old tools that aren't working. This tool, once you learn to use it, helps you to lead yourself as you influence and lead others.

Permission also has its place. Sometimes we need to ask for permission and other times we need to give permission. Often, though, we give our power away when it comes to growth and the pursuit of life by allowing others to dictate our direction. How might our lives be different if we took that power back and were BOLD enough to give permission to ourselves?

Here's a short list of the boldness offered to us:

- Boldness to be our true selves
- Boldness to set healthy boundaries in our relationships
- Boldness to breathe, have fun, and enjoy the journey
- Boldness to find our purpose and share our message
- Boldness to lead others and help them in their journey

I captured some thoughts about permission from people through interviews. Here are some of the questions and a few of the responses:

Question: *Where in your life do you need to give yourself more permission?*

Responses: *Taking time for myself, having a time and space that are my own, expressing myself, embracing where I am, being okay with making mistakes, stop beating myself up, taking better care of myself, learning to let go, being myself, forgiving and accepting myself, making a difference.*

Question: *Why haven't you given yourself permission to do certain things in your life?*

Responses: *Fear, guilt, it takes more time away from family, can't afford it, there's a lot of pressure to achieve in our society, I'll feel like a failure if I don't get things done, I want to fit in with others' expectations, too much effort, supposed to be there for everyone else first, difficulty asking for help, some people will view me as lazy, it seems wasteful.*

Question: *How might your life be different if you gave yourself permission more often?*

Responses: *Happier, relaxed, free, liberated, available for significant things, grateful, more energy, increased inner peace, more creativity, satisfied, relaxed, valuable, whole, a life of joy, I'd love and appreciate those around me more.*

Imagine the impact you would have on yourself and other people if you gave yourself permission to be the best you. Or permission to try something new. Permission to dream, to be happy, acknowledge your feelings, and to create.

I've experienced that one of the first steps to living boldly and more intentionally is giving yourself permission. It's about taking small, deliberate steps to creating the unique life you were meant to have. It's recognizing that the life you are to live is not based on someone else's ideas or approval -- it's based on yours and yours alone!

Think back on a goal, decision, or idea you followed through. You wanted it, you were open to it, and you were "all in." Now think of another goal or change you wanted to make, but you hesitated or you pushed it away because you didn't think it would work out or others wouldn't be supportive of it.

Are there still goals and dreams on your list you believe you're called to do? If so, why haven't you pursued them? Be honest with yourself. Could it be possible you are still playing "Mother May I?" What are some of the factors that prevent you from moving ahead?

Here's a list of a few common factors that prevent people from pursuing their dreams:

- **External Factors:** Lack of support, disapproval from a loved one or a friend, or obligations and demands placed on you

- **Internal Factors:** Fear of failure, fear of disappointment, guilt, a belief in a lie about yourself, lack of balance in your life and priorities, the pull you feel to care for your family even if it's at your own expense, a rigid mindset, a limitation or label

Can you see why permission is a big deal? Too often we're giving away our power by seeking permission and approval from other people, or we withhold permission from ourselves.

How It All Started

One of my mentors, Paul Martinelli, helped me see a little more clearly how this pattern of seeking permission was programmed into us in our youth. We sought it from our parents, teachers, and other authorities. They, usually with good intent, required us to ask permission to either keep us safe or to maintain order. Think about some of the things that required permission that reinforced this mindset. Do you remember asking some of these questions?

- *Can I have a cookie?*

- *May I go outside to play?*

- *May I go to the bathroom?*

- *Is it okay to go to so-and-so's house?*

- *Can I wear this to school?*

- *May I stay up late?*

For every question asked, we were told "yes" or "no." It is a responsible thing for a parent or teacher to protect us, and it makes sense for a child to ask for permission to learn smart choices. But this is where things get wonky. Years later, we don't seek a "yes" or "no" for permission's sake. We seek the validation that permission gives. Validation from those we care about, from our peers and colleagues, even those we barely know. We have a strong innate desire for connection with others, and we long to know we belong and we matter. Many people live with a desire to be validated by others because their own self-validation isn't enough.

As children, we wanted to please our parents and teachers. Our validation was dependent on how they saw us. Our authority figures were happy when we complied and unhappy when we didn't. The way they showed their approval and disapproval shaped our self-image and our course of direction.

As adults, we have to change this learned pattern of thinking. If not, we won't form a confident and healthy image of ourselves. We continually seek the approval of others like we did as children. It is often why some people get caught up in overachieving and striving to prove themselves, or why some will take the opposite approach and shrink back and play small.

Many people experience resistance whenever they try to move beyond their current situation if they haven't given themselves permission. They misinterpret the resistance they feel as a sign they're not supposed to move forward. Instead, they wait for the right time, the right sign, or the right person to give them the green light. It's as if they are still playing the game, but they're afraid to ask: "Mother, may I take one giant step toward my dream?" They fear the answer will be "no." And most often, when we're afraid our answer might be "no," we'll hesitate to even ask the question.

However, when we take back our power and give ourselves permission to live fully and move forward regardless of outside validation, that's when transformation takes place. It doesn't mean all the planets will align in our favor. It means we can create something new and our view of the world opens up. New people come into our path and often our circumstances change.

If we don't permit ourselves to explore and discover what our lives could be, we'll keep rationalizing why our life of playing small is okay and we'll live it, minimizing everything about ourselves, including our gifts and strengths. We'll believe this is just how life is supposed to be, or that these are the cards that were dealt to us.

We'll come up with very logical reasons, yet limiting thinking keeps us from living our best lives.

Here are a few common rational reasons I've heard or I've used:

- *I'll wait until my kids leave home one day.*

- *My job responsibilities require too much of me.*

- *I don't have the time or money.*

- *I'm not smart or healthy enough.*

- *It's too hard.*

- *It's too risky and not practical.*

We can choose to believe these, but if they impede us from developing our potential, it can lead to internal stagnation because we've refused to give our talents and dreams life. We create our own resistance, and then we blame the roles we hide behind. This can lead to resentment. We look for reasons (such as obligation and duty) because this is the "right thing to do" or that's what's "socially acceptable." We look for others to agree with us and might even find the perfect scripture verse to back it up.

Paul Martinelli also told me, "Nothing good grows from the soil of fear and obligation." Whenever we've given someone else the power to give us validation and we don't boldly step into who we were created to be, we're withholding our God-given talents from the world. We're robbing the world of our unique imprint that can provide life-changing opportunities for others. It's our birthright to live abundantly, and it's also our responsibility to share and grow the gifts we've been given.

There is the Parable of the Talents in the Bible where a master put his servants in charge of his money (or talents) while he went away on a trip [1]. When the master returned, he found that two of the servants invested in his talents and the value increased, but the last servant dug a hole in the ground and buried the money.

He rewarded the first two servants according to how well they had invested in his money. The servant who played it safe was thrown out by the master.

This story has great meaning to me and is largely what fuels me to invest in my growth. For years I didn't know what many of my talents or gifts were, and the few I knew I didn't use. I buried them. I had lots of unfulfilled potential and wasted a lot of time and missed many opportunities because I didn't believe I was equipped or prepared to take them on.

I'm guessing you know someone like that too, someone you see with lots of potential but who has never used it or doesn't believe in themselves. Perhaps you've felt that way about your own life, and that there are still things inside you that are waiting to be discovered. Allowing yourself to be open to things inside you will help begin the process of embracing and investing in your growth.

Carpe Diem (Seize the Moment)

Imagine being invited to the beautiful island of Bora Bora located 2,550 miles south of Hawaii in the Pacific Ocean. When you arrive, you start down to the pathway leading to a pristine beach. Would you stop where the pathway meets the sand and wait for someone to give you permission to access the beach? Or, would you step forward and press your toes into the sand or go for a dip in the mesmerizing turquoise water?

The answer is easy, right? You would put your toes in the sand or run to the water! This scenario should make us wonder: If we don't need to seek permission for what we do on our vacation, why do we need to seek permission for what we choose for our vocation?

Or for sharing our strengths to benefit others? Or for loving ourselves or embracing the fullness of life?

I realize that sometimes we are called and required to care for and be responsible for others, whether it's our employees, family, or community. Yes, there are exceptions, but let's not hide behind those roles and accept them as our only mission in life. There is life beyond our current season and we don't have to limit ourselves to only one season.

Saying "yes" to you and to the dreams in your heart is embracing what God planned for your life, no matter where you are. Recognizing your commitment to living boldly also helps those around you—those that only you can impact in the unique way that only you can. Therefore, it is your birthright to live your dream.

It's been said man's pursuit of his dream is what ignites a fire in others. History has proven this. Just look at the lives of Jesus, Gandhi, Martin Luther King Jr., Nelson Mandela, and Mother Teresa. Some of them didn't understand or fulfill their calling until later in life, but once it was clear, they devoted everything to fulfilling it. We can give ourselves permission to do the same even if we don't have full clarity. We can start today, one small step at a time, to seize the moments in front of us—even if we do it imperfectly or awkwardly, which is usually how it starts!

But I get it. Perhaps you're at a time in your life where you want to discover more beyond your current circumstances, but you feel stuck and aren't sure which direction to go. It could be that you're overwhelmed by your situation and you don't see the moment to seize. Or you live in fear of what will happen to those for whom you're responsible if you choose to seize the moment.

If the idea of living boldly is overwhelming for you, remember the quote by Lao Tzu: "The journey of a thousand miles begins with one step." You may not realize it, but each step contains boldness; it requires you to do something you haven't done before. The message here is that any task, however big or small, begins with one discrete action.

If you are apprehensive about taking bold steps, even small ones, you're not alone. I've felt that way before and I've coached people who have both excitement and fear about growing their business and changing their lives. It's normal, but when you allow your inner bold voice to speak louder than your fears, your doubts, and even your deceptive logic, no matter how itty-bitty the steps are, you will experience growth because it's movement.

Boldness, at a glance, seems big, way out there, grandiose in all its glory. But true boldness isn't external. It begins internally by thinking differently and using your imagination to create something new in your life.

When we allow ourselves to take internal bold steps—starting with the first step, it transforms us from the inside out. The external steps become less fleeting; we are not only achieving, we're becoming a higher version of ourselves. Seizing the moment starts on the inside. This mindset is illustrated in Figure 1.

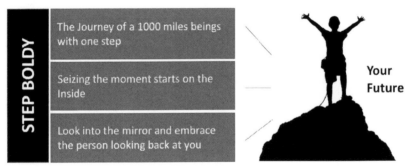

Figure 1 – The Carpe Diem Mindset

Be the Leader

We can't make the impact we were meant to make and seize the moment if we don't pursue our calling and lead ourselves. That's how we attain a joy-filled life. When we do, we grow, transform, and influence those around us.

As you read this book, my biggest hope for you is that you'll use it as a tool to help unlock your voice and unleash the BOLD inside you! Have the courage and bravery to look into the mirror and embrace the person looking back at you—warts and all!

In the chapters that follow, you'll learn about:

- Being yourself and taking off the masks
- Pushing past fear, guilt, and doubt
- Developing new ways of thinking and letting go
- Standing up and embracing your gifts and your mess
- The importance of not rushing the process

At the end of every chapter, there is a quick summary and reflection questions. Keep a journal to capture your thoughts and answers to those questions to enhance your experience. If new ideas form, capture those! Go through this book with a small group or accountability partner to further integrate what you learn into your life.

Decide that whatever comes up while you read, you will commit to taking BOLD steps to be the leader and seize your future. This is about finally claiming the life you've always wanted, guilt-free!

You ARE a gift to the world—and gifts are not meant to remain wrapped. Let's yank the bow, rip the paper, and tear open the box!

It's time to see what's inside you and give yourself permission to be BOLD. So, let's get started on this journey together!

Takeaways

- **Stop playing "Mother May I?"** Don't over-seek validation from others. Give yourself permission to live boldly from the inside out.

- **Don't hide behind roles and responsibilities.** Know when you're playing it "safe" and not living up to your potential.

- **Seize the moment.** Say "yes" to you and to the opportunities in front of you.

- **Be the leader that the world is waiting for.** You are meant to share your growth and empower others.

- **Commit to living boldly.** You decide what "bold" means to you, no matter how big or small the steps are.

Dig Deeper

- What does living "boldly" mean to you?

- Do you sometimes struggle with giving yourself permission? In what areas?

- Why do you think this is a struggle?

- What is not giving yourself permission costing you?

- What would you like to change?

Chapter 2
Be You

Play the lead role in your own story

> *The thing that is really hard, and really*
> *amazing, is giving up on being perfect and*
> *beginning the work of becoming yourself.*

— Anne Quindlen

Has anyone ever told you, "Just be yourself?"

For me, those simple words stand as the biggest, most difficult piece of advice ever given to me by my mom. It's as if she knew when I wasn't being true to myself. And discovering the meaning of those three words would become my life's most challenging pursuit.

Experience Shapes Our Belief

Our beliefs about ourselves are easily shaped and affected by the experiences we face when we are young. One woman I know, let's call her Sam, recalls a trio of experiences that negatively impacted her as a child. These experiences may not be considered traumatic in the world's eyes, but nonetheless created an internal trauma and suffering that would lead to near debilitating fears.

Experience #1

The first experience occurred when Sam was in kindergarten. She remembers being in class and desperately needing to use the bathroom, but her teacher wouldn't let her. She made it clear that they were NOT to talk in class, but Sam really had to "go."

She kept raising her hand, but her teacher demanded she put her hand down. They went back and forth a few times, then things turned into an emergency.

Not wanting to be disobedient, Sam held her bladder as best she could without breaking out into a dance, but it was a losing battle. The worst possible thing in a child's mind at that age happened—an uncomfortable sensation trickled down her pants in front of everyone.

Not yet knowing what had occurred, her teacher eventually came over and said, "Sam, now you may ask your question." But before Sam could respond, her teacher saw the stain and quickly told her to head to the bathroom. Like a scene out of the movie *The Green Mile,* Sam took a long walk across the room in front of her classmates. It was hard not to notice her light brown polyester pantsuit with a dark wet streak going down one leg. For her, that experience was humiliating, and never forgotten.

Experience #2

The second incident was a year later when Sam was in first grade. During class, her sweater kept falling off the back of her chair. Each time, she picked it up off the floor, but it was a distraction for the teacher. Finally, the teacher got annoyed with Sam.

While taking her sweater away could have rectified the situation, this particular teacher's standard method of punishment was to put a misbehaved student in a closet. And that's precisely what she did with Sam. This closet was behind the other students' desks in a small, separate room. Inside this cramped space was a little wooden desk, some school supplies, and a light.

Sam recalls how separated she felt from everyone in the class. She shared, "It was as if my teacher wanted to send a message that I didn't deserve to be with everyone else. I felt shunned."

While Sam wasn't the only child who was put in the closet that year, she developed the faulty belief that she was bad and deserved to be punished. She felt she was a bother to her teacher, classmates, and everyone else. Her greatest desire was to fit in and feel accepted, but she felt alone and insignificant.

Experience #3

The third incident for Sam was in third grade. Her teacher was well-liked by everyone, including Sam. She recounts, "Miss Taylor was everyone's favorite and they loved her. She was sweet, and she was pretty." Sam often looked to her for direction and trusted her implicitly.

One particular day, though, Miss Taylor asked the class a very deep question, "If you're a Christian, please raise your hand." At that point in life, Sam wasn't quite sure if she was, and since she believed it was more important to be honest, she didn't raise her hand.

To her surprise, she was the only one in the class who didn't have an extended hand. Everyone stared at her wide-eyed. She heard someone say, "Oh my gosh, you're not a Christian?" For Sam, that moment was haunting. She immediately felt shame and guilt. "I felt I had done something unforgivable, and it validated my belief that I didn't fit in and I didn't have a right to be there."

Miss Taylor, in her sweet voice, spoke up. "Now, class, let's all support Samantha and pray for her." Soon after, the teacher told the principal, who met with Sam and impressed upon her how important it was for her to be a Christian. He instructed her to go home and get "right" with God.

The next day Miss Taylor asked Sam "the question." "Samantha, do you have something you want to share with the class?" She slowly stood up and told the class that she became a Christian the night before.

Everybody clapped, but instead of feeling happy, Sam felt something deeply wrong inside. She couldn't put it into words at the time, but it didn't feel genuine. She felt dishonest because she did it only to please others and make her teacher happy. Instead of feeling like she now fit in, she felt even more isolated. From that point on, Sam built up walls to keep others from getting too close in fear that she would eventually disappoint them and they would reject her.

Sam I Am

As you contemplate Sam's story, consider what kind of impact that triad of experiences had on her—especially at such a tender age. Also, what do you think the odds were of her finding a way to rise above it? Impossible? Difficult? Easy?

Well, the answer to that question is that it was difficult for her, but fortunately not impossible. And I can tell you why I know. It's because Sam is me. These experiences completely altered my view of myself, God, life, and all the people in it.

Learning How to Be Yourself

My story is in no way unique. Yes, there are worse things that could happen. Yet, we all respond uniquely to pain and trauma, depending on various factors. One of those factors is how resilient we are, which I will cover in an upcoming chapter. When we experience any pain that negatively impacts how we see ourselves and the world, it can dictate how we live our lives. Some find a way to rise above it, others struggle to cope with it.

Even though those experiences affected how I lived for many years, the good news is that I am a different person today. With the help of God, friends, and family, I found a way through it, and those experiences made me stronger. I want to encourage you, if you are still struggling with pain from your past, no matter how deep it runs, you can rise above it too! It doesn't mean you'll forget it, or that it won't ever come up again, but there is a way through it.

Looking back at those painful times of my childhood allows me to understand more of what was going through my mind at that time.

The first incident I mentioned was humiliating, although I wasn't able to describe it that way until years later. Imagine having to go to the bathroom and asking for permission to do something that is a basic need, but you feel you have no right to ask for it. Now I'm certain if the teacher really knew what was happening, she would have granted me permission. But because of how I perceived my life at the time, I felt like I had no right to speak up for myself. Shortly after that situation, my Mom began to encourage me almost daily with a set of words I'll never forget. She would tell me, "Barbie, just be yourself." The only problem was, I didn't know how because I didn't know who I was.

The second experience was also humiliating. Despite the fact that teachers today wouldn't get by with putting a student in a closet, it was at that point I started fading into the background and became a wallflower to keep from annoying people. But again my Mom would encourage me, "Just be yourself!" My problem, though, was I still didn't know how. I found it easier to be a quiet good little girl than to risk speaking up and getting into trouble.

The third experience somehow solidified my previous experiences and beliefs. I was torn between pleasing others—my mom, my teacher, my principal, and my classmates—and being true to myself. Because I wanted to be accepted, I defaulted to trying to make others happy instead of feeling my own happiness. I had a few friends, but I constantly worried they would eventually get mad at me and see me as a misfit. I felt uncomfortable in my own skin. It felt like the world that I lived in wasn't allowing me to be myself.

It wasn't until years later that I finally learned to break away from this prison and give myself permission—the permission to be me. What a glorious feeling it is to feel free to be yourself! Allowing myself to let my true self come through has allowed me to step boldly and discover the life that had always been waiting for me.

I now recognize that those self-defeating thoughts—that I wasn't good enough, I was a bad person, I was unlovable—were actually reflections of what I believed about myself. Permission exposed that the negative thoughts I *believed* others had about me were lies I repeatedly told myself. Isn't it interesting how we will be committed to thinking the same thoughts over and over, even if they are based on lies?

The Power of a Seed

Those former words "just be yourself" from my mom's lips turned out to be seeds of hope that were planted in my heart. Years later, those same seeds eventually sprouted and started to grow. I wish she were still here so that she could see the fruits of her belief in me. I think she sensed how much I wanted to fit in and connect with others. She saw me as I truly was, a unique blend of God's handiwork, which was quite different than how I saw myself—as an awkward, ugly, tall, skinny girl.

I remember my mom saying to me occasionally, "You really need to start speaking up and standing up for yourself. Take responsibility for YOU." At that time, trying to gain people's approval was less painful than trying to stand up for myself. I was far more invested in the image of who I thought I was supposed to be than who I really was—a fun, quirky, free-spirited girl who loved to dance to anything and be creative.

Looking back, my mom wasn't the only one who planted seeds in me; there were other teachers who saw my strengths, believed in me, and even went out of their way to encourage me. One of the biggest gifts you can give someone is believing in them and telling them you believe in them, even if they don't believe in themselves yet.

Later, as I became more aware of how my faulty beliefs limited me, I was determined to uncover the true me. I wanted it more than winning the lottery. I wish I could tell you there was a pill, a switch, or a quick fix that I discovered, but there wasn't. It wasn't a one-time goal I achieved. Instead, it's been an unfolding process of discovery. I've made lots of headway, but I'm still on that journey. And it started with the power of a seed that simply needed to take root.

Who planted seeds inside of you when you were growing up? Have they taken root yet? If not, don't be disheartened; sometimes they take a while. But once they do, look out! There will come a point in time when they will begin to take off and grow into something more than you could have ever imagined!

Challenge Your Current Paradigm

If you ever struggle with being yourself or know someone who does, never give up! True self is not found in fixing yourself, but rather in loving and accepting yourself because you have great value.

As for me, just when I think I've mastered it, I still sometimes slip back into my old thinking. The more I stretch and grow, the more I unlearn and find other parts of myself that are waiting to emerge. I've learned to love the younger version of me, the one who didn't stand up for herself. She was brave and had guts for not raising her hand when she could have!

Being willing to ask ourselves questions that challenge our thinking is a subtle yet bold step in forming new beliefs about our self and the world. Being your true self can be scary at first, especially if you don't like to stand out or you fear what others may think of you. But once you start taking these steps to discover who you really are and give life to that part of you a little more every day, you have already begun the process.

The Bold Version of You

What does that bold version of you look like? Have you ever thought about that? You know, the part of you that is unstoppable? Maybe you are like me and don't have the kind of personality that others would consider bold. Even though I love people, I'm more of an introvert. Many in our society envision BOLD as being more extroverted or someone who has a more outgoing personality. I think hogwash! It's inside ALL of us to be bold; it just looks different from one person to the next.

Take a moment to define what BOLD means to you. No one can tell you exactly what BOLD looks like. Ultimately, you have to tailor it to yourself. I can, however, offer a few pointers. I call these the "Steps to Unlearning," which are illustrated in Figure 2. What we need to do is unlearn old ways and develop new ways. Think of these as breaking old habits that hold you back and replacing them with new habits that will help you discover your true self!

OLD WAYS	NEW WAYS
• Obeying Every Expectation	• Getting to Know Yourself
• Taking Unselfish to the Extreme	• Releasing Yourself From Other People's Stories
• Depending on Your Masks	• Using the Word "No" More Often

Figure 2 – The Steps to Unlearning

Old Way - Obey Every Expectation

Growing up, I wanted more than anything to obey the rules, please whomever I was around, and honor those in positions of authority. Unfortunately, I took it to the extreme and did this even when it was harmful to me. I would see things as black or white, either/or, all-or-nothing, right or wrong. I was a concrete thinker with very few shades of gray.

In my experience in kindergarten, most children would have challenged the teacher, excused themselves, or just blurted out, "I have to pee!" But not me. I was determined to follow the rules, even if it meant ignoring my bladder!

There are times we need to challenge situations and not oblige external expectations when our character, values, or boundaries are crossed. We need to be advocates for ourselves and take care of our needs. If we wait for others to advocate for us, it may never happen. If we don't take care of us, we will be less equipped to help others.

Old Way - Take Unselfish to the Extreme

Often, we view people as either selfish or unselfish. Yet, when we put people into only these two categories, we are thinking from a black and white mindset. We judge ourselves or fear what others may think of us if we want to do something for ourselves.

Being unselfish doesn't mean that (a) we have to totally ignore who we are, or (b) we need to always place the needs of others before our own, or (c) we need the approval of others to live our life and pursue our dreams.

The beautiful thing about giving ourselves permission to take care of our own needs is that we can become a fountain from which we can give back to others. We've all heard the oxygen mask example; you don't put the mask on yourself last, you put it on first. The same is true for helping to save someone from drowning. You put on a life jacket first, otherwise the person you're helping may cause you both to drown.

While we are led to believe that it is noble to always put others first, there is nothing honorable about doing it at the expense of our own health and burning out. Studies show we are much happier and healthier emotionally *and* physically, and we can give more, when we first take care of ourselves. I know for me, I'm able to give more when I take care of myself. Sometimes I'm no good to anyone unless I take care of my core basic needs first. I bet you are wired the same way. This is where we need give ourselves permission to put on the oxygen mask first -- to put on that life jacket. That way we can help others.

Focusing on your needs might be uncomfortable at first like it was for me. Here are several reminders that give me perspective when I'm tempted to only put other people's needs first (Note: Yes, sigh, I still have to remind myself.):

- Taking care of my needs helps me to be more resourceful to others.

- Frequently giving back to myself increases my hunger to pay it forward.

- Having self-love and compassion gives me more love and compassion for others.

Some may say focusing on your own needs is selfish. I view it as being more centered and at peace, and everyone around you can benefit.

No longer do we need to believe that we're either selfish or unselfish. Yes, we get off-balance from time to time, but it doesn't *make* us selfish. As one of my mentors, John C. Maxwell, shares, "You cannot give what you do not have." If you're running on empty, you will exhaust your ability to give. If you take care of yourself and fill yourself up often, you can better take care of others.

Old Way – Depend on Your Masks

We all have a story—many, in fact. Stories of our childhood, accomplishments, challenges, and celebrations. These are all held in our memory, many linked to strong positive or negative emotions. Some stories lift us up, others keep us playing small. Often, we don't recognize the stories that limit us.

Which story we believe, the B.S. or the Real Story, can either empower us or disempower us.

Our B.S. Story

One of my mentors coined this as our Bogus Story, and it's very fitting [1]. The B.S. is a story that can have some facts embedded in it, but that we've added our own meaning to—often negative and limiting, or exaggerating—or we've adopted someone else's interpretation. Sometimes our own Belief System can also be a Bogus Story.

Our Real Story

This is the story that we tell ourselves that contains facts about our experiences combined with our core values. While it isn't always roses and unicorns, it is empowering and authentic, and we get to be our true selves. We recognize our own resourcefulness, and also our limits. This story creates a positive vision for our lives and contains our message, purpose, and what we desire for ourselves and others.

Let's get back to the B.S. (it's appropriately named, right?). When we don't tell ourselves our true or real story, we feel misaligned, even though we can't put our thumb on the reason as to why. Instead, the truth is masked with a persona, essentially a mask, that helps us make sense of something and makes us feels "safer." But it's just another Bogus Story in disguise that has hidden our true masterpiece, our self. We settle for an ordinary "normal" copy and forfeit our uniqueness. But B.S. is B.S. until you change it.

I've traded my true self for masks over the years. I didn't consciously think, "Oh, I'm going to go and put my mask on now." I just didn't know how to be my true self, so I grabbed onto whatever was comfortable and available at the time—a mask of being a good girl, someone who looked like they had it all together. It was something I could control.

There are still times I default into "mask mode" and buy into the old belief that it will protect me from rejection. Sometimes it's easier to put on a sweet smile than to admit I feel lonely.

Here's the thing: When we put on a mask, we're not just afraid of others seeing who we really are, we're actually hiding from ourselves. By hiding, we block ourselves from seeing our value and how much God loves us even on our worst days.

One of the hardest masks for me to take off is the "Mask of Perfection." Sometimes I'm still afraid of letting others see that I have insecurities, fears, and weaknesses. While we know it's impossible to be perfect, we still try! We're fooling no one but ourselves. As long as we allow ourselves to be tricked by our own minds, like the movie *The Mask* with Jim Carrey, the mask somehow finds its way onto our face no matter how hard we try to pull it off.

I'm learning that the more I let my guard down and let others see me, imperfections and all, the more I am at ease with myself and people. It's allowing me to connect more and believe I DO belong. I AM safe. When I am willing to let others see me for my true self, I'm silently inviting them to do the same.

Taking off a mask can be hard at first, especially if it feels like it's been super-glued on. So, if you're working on this area, don't expect it to come off immediately. Be gentle with yourself.

Be prepared to have some pain surface, and also be ready to see yourself in a completely new light. I began to see the wonderful parts, the ugly parts, and everything in between. And for the first time, I saw myself as my mom saw me and began to get glimpses of how God sees me.

"Holy crap! Me?" I thought. *"I have something to offer the world? I don't have to feel ashamed?"* This revelation sparked a fire in me that has never left.

I reached out to trusted friends and asked people to mentor me. I asked them what strengths and qualities they saw in me. I desperately wanted to believe in myself. There were times I wanted to quit because it seemed like it was taking forever, but people around me kept encouraging me to never stop.

Then I began to love myself. I initially thought it was the most selfish thing I could do, but little by little I began loving myself and thanking God for how He made me. The interesting thing that happened—I began to love God and others more.

I can now walk by a mirror and say without hesitation, "Girl… you got it going on!" or "You are rocking that outfit!" or "Go kick some ass today!" This girl has come a long way!

After learning to get real and vulnerable with myself, I now recognize when I'm tempted to put my mask back on or when it goes up automatically. Now I don't try to fight it, I embrace it. Here's how I sometimes coach myself through it:

- I recognize what I'm doing and say to myself, "Isn't that interesting, the mask is back!" Then I refrain from self-judgment and internally acknowledge that eventually the mask will come off again; it's only temporary.

- I recognize my responsibility and that I can choose something different. If I choose to keep the mask on in that moment, I accept it and own my decision at that time.

- I show myself compassion and honor my choice, knowing I can re-choose something else later.

- I acknowledge the boldness it took to face that situation and recommit to keep letting the real me come through no matter what it takes, even if it's one baby step at a time.

Taking off our masks doesn't have to be a fight. We don't have to rip them off. We can coax them to come down, or we can choose to wear them for a while. The key is to be aware of them and don't let them have the final say.

New Way – Get to Know Yourself

Most of us have a very different view of who we are versus how others see us and how our Creator sees us. Eric Hoffer once said, "No matter what our achievements might be, we think well of ourselves only in rare moments. We need people to bear witness against our inner judge, who keeps book on our shortcomings and transgressions. We need people to convince us that we are not as bad as we think we are." While I agree with most of this statement, I would change that we need to convince *ourselves* that we are not as bad as we think we are. We don't need to wait for others to tell us. We can become such strong advocates of ourselves that we don't need to wait for validation from others.

How can we convince ourselves that we aren't as bad as we think we are? For starters, get to know yourself. How well do you know yourself? I'm talking about *really* knowing yourself. Knowing how and why you tick, what motivates you, excites you, saps you?

Questions like these allow you to boldly go places where you haven't gone before (yes, I was a Star Trek fan!). If you want to really know yourself, you need to be willing to go deep.

When I was younger, I fished a lot. Occasionally, I would get a nibble, and if I got lucky I would catch something along the banks. But the deep water was where the real action was. On a rare occasion, I would venture further out on a boat, and with the right lure and bait I would catch fish that I could never catch along the shore.

You may not like to fish, but I share this story to emphasize a core point. If you want to discover more about yourself, you won't find much in the shallow water. Think about people who only ask "surface" or chitchat questions; we often say they are, well, shallow.

Going deep requires being BOLD. We may not know what might be uncovered; *yes*, there is a risk, yet something more meaningful inside starts taking place. You'll start having more questions about life, yourself, and your dreams. When you start asking these questions, expect to start getting answers. In fact, answers usually don't come unless you ask. When you do ask, you'll be met with more clarity and often new ideas that are waiting to be unlocked.

On the flip side, you'll also have other things rise to the surface; sometimes pain, sadness, and fears—the not-so-fun stuff. Just know that this is part of the process of your life beginning to uncover the real, beautiful, brave, and bold you. Embrace it all.

New Way – Release Yourself from Other People's Stories

Sometimes we get attached to other people's victim stories and feel we need to be part of it. This was a pattern that showed up for me in many of my relationships. I recognized it when I began coaching. I attracted desperate people who wanted help, but they didn't take responsibility for their lack of success. They were drawn to me, in part, because I was a good listener and compassionate and would offer to always be there for them.

I would let them dump and dump and dump…all over me. As you can imagine, it worked out great for them. For me, it was draining, and I wondered if I had the energy to continue coaching. Eventually I realized the problem wasn't them, it was me! I had allowed them to do this.

Once I started releasing myself from their stories, and became clear on who I *wanted* to work with, my mindset changed. I started setting clear boundaries for myself. Instead of taking on clients who excessively complained, I now only work with those who are purpose-driven, and excited about growth and doing the work, not just those wanting a quick fix to their situation. I went from feeling fried to feeling energized (sounds like a snazzy title for a blog, doesn't it?).

New Way – Understand the Power of "No"

I'm naturally a peacemaker and someone who has a lot of empathy; I don't like conflict. I used to think it was wrong to say "no." I didn't understand that conflict could actually be a healthy opportunity to improve a relationship and bring people closer together.

I discovered that "no" can be a very empowering word and can allow you to say "yes" to something that is aligned with your purpose. Saying "no" will be hard at first. It takes lots of practice.

When you learn to be clear without feeling you need to give an explanation…oh my, look out! Saying "no" can be one of the most freeing things you can do for yourself, but be prepared for pushback. I've seen many people feel trapped in decisions because they were afraid to say "no" to a friend, or they felt it was their duty, or they feared someone would think they were selfish. Give yourself permission to release yourself from other people's stories or what you think they're thinking. Give yourself permission to rewrite your story. Saying "no" is a good place to start!

•••

Learning who you are and giving yourself permission to live life on your own terms can be a lifelong process. But once you've started, tell your story and pursue a life of boldness!

If you know others around you who struggle with being themselves, believe in them, and treat them as if they have already stepped into that belief. Often, taking the focus off of trying so hard to be yourself gives you the energy to focus on what you are already creating. Bob Goff, who wrote *Love Does*, said, "Quit letting who you were talk you out of who you're becoming." [2]

For a long time, I lived with regret for not letting my true self show. Now, instead of getting frustrated at what I don't yet see, I focus on who I'm *becoming*. I don't regret what I had to go through; it's shaped me into who I am today, and now I'm able to help others who have struggled with the same issues. Sometimes we have to totally lose ourselves before we find ourselves.

Recognize that you already have everything inside you—it may require some exploring, hard work, and cleaning up, but it's there! You were created for a unique purpose; not just to exist, but also to create change in the world. No one can do it like you can!

Takeaways

- **Be yourself.** You were made to live a purpose designed just for you.

- **Don't obey every expectation.** A *pleasing others* mentality sets you up to a life of self-misalignment.

- **Don't take unselfish to the extreme.** It's noble to want to put others first, but it's healthy to choose yourself too.

- **Don't live behind a mask.** Masks are comfortable, but you weren't meant to hide your true self.

- **Get to know yourself.** Learn who you really are and be willing to go deep to discover it.

- **Release yourself from other people's stories.** Give yourself permission to not give an audience to—or participate in—every person's story.

- **Understand the power of "no".** When you have more clarity about who you are and your purpose in life, saying "no" becomes easier.

Dig Deeper

- Has there been a time in your life where you struggled with being yourself? How did it affect you?

- What story do you think you were telling that kept you from letting your true self shine through?

- What is a Bogus Story that you're still holding on to? How is it affecting your results now?

- What is a new story you could tell yourself to have a better outcome?

Chapter 3
Push Past

Identify the obstacles keeping you
from being "all in"

We are all faced with a series of
great opportunities brilliantly disguised as
impossible situations.

— Chuck Swindoll

Some aspects of life are simply not in our control. We may be able to pick our friends and our career, but we don't get to pick our parents, our country, our race, or our culture. And sometimes we don't like what life gives us. The best we can do is seek guidance, see what we can change, and overcome challenges that we face. But the question is HOW? How can we take what life gives us, and know which parts to embrace, surrender, or change?

The best story I know that exemplifies this lesson is the story of my mom, who has always inspired me. I like to say she not only knew how to turn lemons into lemonade, she loved teaching others how to make their own. Her life, like yours and mine, had purpose. But she had to discover it for herself.

Rising from the Cotton Fields

My mom, Peggie Sue, or "Little Peg" as many called her, was the youngest of fifteen children. She, her parents, and her siblings lived on the outskirts of Sledge, Mississippi, where they picked cotton on a 60-acre plantation owned by a wealthy landowner. They were sharecroppers.

Sledge is just a blip on the map, and at the time my mom lived there, the population was less than a whopping 500 people. She and her family would work the fields, planting, hoeing, and picking cotton. The cotton season was early May through November, when the last of cotton was harvested.

The shack my mom and her family lived in had four simple rooms—a kitchen with a black potbellied stove for cooking and heat, a living room, a bedroom, and a back room. They also had one feature that few houses today have to offer—an outhouse. Imagine a large family of seventeen living in a modest shack and competing for the use of the outhouse (and toilet paper!).

By the time my mom was five, some of the sisters and brothers had married and moved on, but it was still a tight fit, making the remaining family feel like they were packed in like a can of sardines.

Each year the landowner paid them a small "settlement" (usually around $500), sometimes considerably less if they owed any rent. It was always a big day for everyone when "settlement" came. They would go into town together and each family member would buy one article of clothing. My mom would always get a bag of hard candy and apples. She ate every part of the apple except the stem. I still remember to this day her eating apples, core and all. She didn't like to see things go to waste.

When mom was nine, her daddy passed away. After his death, life became even harder. She had to work the cotton fields from sun up to sun down and couldn't attend school until the cotton season was over, yet she was still expected to turn in assignments and keep up her grades.

She said that often things would take a toll on my grandmother, who was now a single parent raising a large family and in charge of making sure she could feed the family and still get the work done.

As a child, my mom heard the phrase, "You should be ashamed of yourself," repeatedly spoken to her. This left a strong impression on her, and for years she struggled with shame of who she was and where she came from. Yet she found a way to quiet that voice and give herself permission to be BOLD and find the new life that was waiting for her.

When mom turned 13, my grandmother went on welfare and was able to move the family into their first "real" house for $25 a month. Even though they were no longer working the cotton fields, life was still hard. Their main diet was now pinto beans and potatoes. Occasionally, if they were fortunate, they would get a can of mackerel to split between them all.

The best part of their move, from the outskirts of Sledge to the middle of town, was that my mom could start school in September of each year. She did well academically but still felt stigmatized, as everyone knew they were poor.

Mom wanted desperately to leave and find a new life away from the roots that had enslaved her, so graduating from high school was high on her list. She sometimes felt there was no way out, but kept clinging to hope. During her senior year, she developed a strong faith in God and sensed He had a greater plan for her life.

After mom graduated, she found the courage to leave the little town of Sledge and headed for Memphis. While she feared stepping into a world of the unknown, it was nothing compared to the pain from her childhood.

I admire the boldness my mom had. Despite her external challenges, she didn't allow what she experienced—poverty on many sides—to have power over her mind. It's easy to be consumed by difficult experiences and poverty when that's all you've known. But one doesn't have to go through these experiences to be influenced by a poverty mindset. A poverty mindset believes that things are the way they are and will never change. That they will be as they have always been. A poverty mindset has you thinking that you will never have enough or be enough.

When those become the predominant thoughts in our minds, we're not able to see the opportunities in front of us. Everything becomes a competition; we compare ourselves to others, and in our minds, we never measure up. With abundance thinking, it doesn't mean we have to always think positive, but we believe there is enough for everyone, including us, even if we can't currently see it yet.

For many years my mom was in "survival mode," from the time she was born until she graduated from high school. There were many days she went hungry and lived in fear that the family would lose their house. Thankfully, she felt a hope inside her that there was more possibility and she was determined to find a way to thrive no matter how long it took. Eventually she fulfilled her lifetime dream of becoming a nurse and lived her life to the fullest in the best way she knew how.

Despite her challenges, mom never made excuses. She gave herself permission to live her life differently, breaking away from generational poverty and a defeatist mindset. Even though she is no longer with us, I clearly remember how she pushed past obstacles. The way she lived her life challenges me daily to do the same and I desire the same for you.

Overcoming the Obstacles

Obstacles can either keep us from growth or help us to grow; the result is based on our response. Obstacles are a part of life, but they don't have to consume us or keep us from living fully. Even the obstacles that seem insurmountable can be turned into stepping stones that lead us towards growth. But in order to see them as stepping stones, we need to get clear about which ones are keeping us from moving forward. Common obstacles we face are illustrated in Figure 3.

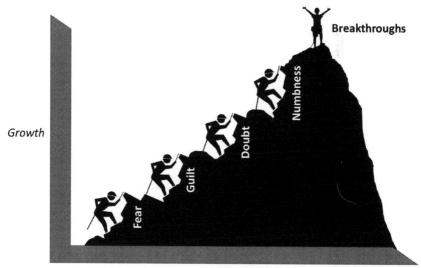

Figure 3 – The Common Obstacles We Face

Obstacle #1: Fear

My mom had many great qualities, but, like everyone, she had weaknesses. One of hers was fear—fear of drowning, fear of rejection, fear of losing people that were important to her.

Many people have these same fears and more. So where does fear come from? Some argue it's "natured or nurtured" into us, some say it's a spiritual battle happening inside of us. In my own life, I've experienced all of these to be true.

I've always been fascinated with how the mind, body, and brain work together, especially when it comes to dealing with fears, mostly because I wanted to overcome my own. Our limbic system, a.k.a. "lizard brain," naturally alerts us to dangerous situations, and when it does, it overrides the reasoning part of our brain [1]. Thank goodness it does, because if it didn't and we were about to be attacked by a lion, we wouldn't recognize we were even in danger.

But all too often, fear shows up in non-dangerous situations and can hijack our nervous system, responding as if we need to freeze or flee. We get stuck in "high alert" and aren't able to come down into a state of calm or think rationally. This can be caused by many factors including trauma, chronic stress, learned habits, limiting beliefs and even some brain injuries.

One of my greatest fears was speaking in public, which was very likely imprinted on me from those three early childhood experiences I shared in Chapter 1. I did not know how to cope and process the shame and humiliation I felt, so it continued to show up in other areas. I began to see the world as a scary place, so I avoided being in new situations and unfamiliar people whenever I could.

I think God had a sense of humor when he planted the seed in my heart to become a coach and speaker. I've since found that what we're most afraid of can actually lead us to finding our unique purpose in life.

I'm not saying we all need to go out and become speakers, write a book, or go bungee jumping. But we are all meant for growth, and if we allow our fears to have power over us, the gifts we've been given aren't able to be used in full capacity. In other words, we can't be "all in". Only by facing our fears can find ourselves and discover what we're truly capable of doing.

So how do we begin to overcome our fears? There is a lot of great advice out there. I'm going to share what helped me, but ultimately you have to be willing to find what works for you. Think of this more as a guide. It begins by exploring and asking yourself the right questions to decide your next steps.

Embracing Your Fears

A key factor that helps me overcome my fears (yes, that's present tense) is embracing them. Most people take the opposite approach. They focus on blasting or annihilating them, avoiding them, or seeing fear as their greatest enemy. For me, it's about getting to know and understand my fears and what are the different ways I can respond to them. It's about how I can leverage what I learned to change my experience.

Over time, I've developed a new relationship and conversation with my fears. This alone has taken the pressure off just enough, so I can focus on the boldness and courage I want in that moment.

Does fear still show up? Heck yeah! But now I know what's happening. I take the time I need, and I even quietly thank that fear because I know it's going to teach me something about myself, as long as I'm open to it. The icing on the cake is that the voice of fear no longer has the final say.

Understanding Your Fears

Learning how my mind and brain work and how they impact the rest of my body has lessened its power on me. It no longer seems like a scary monster waiting to devour me. That's what many overwhelming things in life feel like initially—scary. But when we learn more about them and become more familiar with them, the smaller they become.

I recently learned that a mild head injury from a horseback riding accident years earlier was causing my nervous system to over-respond. It was empowering to finally know where some of my anxiety was coming from. Today, I better understand what I can control and what I can't, and ways I can focus my energy to be more productive. You can do the same. Despite all the things you don't have control over, you can choose how you respond to your fears and discomfort.

Often, though, when we face a fear or discomfort, we want to run the other way. In the book *Your Survival Instinct is Killing You: Retrain Your Brain to Conquer Fear and Build Resilience* by Dr. Marc Schoen, he says it's important to accept levels of discomfort [2]. He shares about how our goal should not be to avoid discomfort, but to embrace it so we can build resilience and new thought patterns. There are more and more studies showing that our brains can change and that we can grow new neural pathways; this is called neuroplasticity, and for me this was good news!

You may be reading this thinking, *"I don't experience much or any fear."* Even if you aren't held back by it, I can assure you that there are those around you that are, sometimes every day, you just might not know it. They may put a smile on their face and hide it like I did, but it's still there and it can be debilitating. If you know someone around you that struggles with anxiety or fear, don't try to fix them or tell them to "Just calm down!" or "Get over it." Listen to them, encourage them. Most importantly, let them know that you believe in them and that in the right time they'll find a way to get through it.

When you allow yourself to step out and get uncomfortable despite your fears, living boldly becomes your focus, even if it's one small step at a time. Your confidence will grow, and fear will eventually loosen its grip on you. And *when* it shows up, it will no longer have the final say!

Obstacle #2: Guilt

When I was younger, I was the kid that would turn bright red when you looked at me, even if I had done nothing wrong. I had that "guilty look." It's one thing to feel guilty if you're at fault, but imagine feeling guilty even when you've done nothing wrong.

I felt guilty and responsible when others were upset or hurting, especially when it came to family members. Life at home was challenging, and I took it upon myself, even as a small child, to keep things peaceful for others. I believe this was a form of self-protection to make life less painful for me.

I was afraid of sharing my feelings when I would achieve something. Even though I loved the song "This Little Light of Mine," I was afraid of shining my light, as I didn't want others to feel diminished, and carried this pattern into adulthood.

In my early 40s, I hired a life coach to help me sort out some difficult decisions I needed to make. During one of our sessions, she asked me, "Have you ever heard of survivor's guilt?" She explained that this can exist not just with those who had survived war or natural disasters, but also with people whose parents or siblings have a physical, emotional, or mental challenge. They feel guilty whenever they are doing well in life while their loved ones are suffering. They try not to stand out, for fear they will make their loved one's situation worse.

As I began to examine my relationships with family members, I realized how much it played out in my youth and now that I am older. I used to feel guilty when I achieved something, did something nice for myself or went after a new goal. Today, I'm much better at it, but at times it's still a struggle.

I imagine that at some point in our lives we all struggle with feeling guilt over something. Maybe you put in longer hours at work and feel guilty for not spending enough time with family. Or maybe you want to take time for yourself, but you think other people will think you're selfish. Or maybe you've had a breakthrough and you want to share it with others but don't want to come across as tooting your horn. Or maybe you want to pursue something outside of family but feel it's your duty to take care of everyone else's needs, instead of your own.

Let me share a story about a friend who often struggled with guilt. Stacy's first husband was from a family and culture where they valued excessively what other people thought of them, especially mothers. The women would often worry if other people thought they were "good moms," or if they were raising their children the "right" way, and they almost always put themselves last. This created unhealthy comparisons, especially for Stacy, making her aware of how easy it is to be swallowed up in feelings of inadequacy.

She noticed it in her own upbringing, and recalls that when she was younger her mom would frequently say, "I'm a failure as a mother." This thought became a pattern of thinking for Stacy that caused insecurities and feelings of guilt whenever she did something for herself.

It wasn't until her second marriage, when she moved to a different country, that she realized the influences of culture on different thought patterns. There, many mothers were actually the breadwinners in the family. Many husbands stayed at home and were supportive of their working spouse. The couples found a way to work together, and the working wives seemed to have little guilt. They were much happier, and the family units were strong. Contrast that to other cultures, where a sense of guilt might weigh heavily on a working mom. Guilt like that impacts relationships, and a person's well-being.

Do you sometimes struggle with feelings of guilt that impact the way you want to live? If so, how far back can you remember feeling this way? Was there someone who influenced you to think this way, or was there an experience that triggered this? Guilt can become a leech on living a bold life and thinking abundantly; it will suck the life right out of you.

Obstacle #3: Doubt

I shared earlier that I struggled with believing in myself. I questioned myself over so many little things that it grew into a huge mountain of doubt.

Early in my coaching career, my confidence was very low. I often questioned myself and thought, *"Who am I to help these people when I don't even believe in myself? And, who am I to do this when I'm struggling in the same area?"*

Regardless of these feelings, and despite the doubt, I took action and noticed my confidence beginning to grow. I would say "yes" to opportunities instead of avoiding them. Soon, other people took notice of my growth, and often asked what I was doing different. More exciting was the noticeable growth happening in my clients as a result.

While it's important to live what you're teaching others, I don't believe you need to have it all together. As long as you're intentionally growing and learning you can make an impact. When we put the pressure on ourselves to always have our act together, we doubt ourselves and worry that people will find out we're imperfect. And when they do, we fear they will reject us.

One of the ways doubt shows up is through something called Imposter Syndrome. This affects many people, including professionals, athletes, parents, coaches, counselors, and teachers. It often shows up when people start a new job, build a new skill, begin to realize a dream, or become recognized.

Melanie, a dear friend and business coach, wrote an article on this syndrome entitled "Are You a Fraud?" She shares some examples of the internal dialogue many of us have when we experience Imposter Syndrome [3]:

- How can I be a relationship expert when I'm struggling in a relationship?

- Who am I to help people with their health needs when I'm 20 pounds overweight?

- I've never been in their shoes and don't know what they are going through, why would they trust me?

- My business is struggling, so who am I to market myself as a business coach?

- I'm an introvert and people will question my ability as a speaker.

You get the idea. Thoughts like these can hijack you and keep you from sharing your gifts with the world. It was a relief to realize I didn't have to have all the answers or have all the same experiences or credentials in order to help someone. I just needed to have a desire to help people, be present with them, and ask questions that guide them to listen to their intuition.

I don't believe our beautifully packaged story is what will inspire others; it's our willingness to share our growth in the midst of our doubt.

Obstacle #4: Numbness

When I started to face the pain of my childhood, emotions came flooding in. It caught me off guard. I discovered I had pushed away a lot of unresolved pain. I was a classic stuffer, and whenever anything uncomfortable from my past came up, how did I deal with it? I got busy. I got busy with my career, my family, and volunteering just to avoid and numb the pain that I felt.

In *The Deeper Path: Five Steps That Let Your Hurts Lead to Your Healing*, Kary Oberbrunner shares why numbing our pain also numbs our potential [4]. While we are able to keep our pain at bay, we also deny our strengths and it prevents us from living boldly. It reminds me of the parable that describes how a frog can be easily boiled alive and not even feel the pain. If a frog is suddenly placed into boiling water, it's going to freaking jump out. However, if it is placed in the pot at room temperature and the water is gradually heated to a boil, the frog will not even feel it or be aware that it's being cooked to death.

You and I can be like the frog in the tepid water. We'd rather stay comfortable than deal with life's pain and discomfort. We may not literally die from it, but we can die a slow internal death by not growing and not allowing ourselves to dream. Pain, unreleased, can trap us inside ourselves. Eventually, if not dealt with, it will seep out (or sometimes erupt) and affect our health, relationships, experiences, and ultimately kill our joy.

I've found that, in order to release my pain, I need to go through it. Not around, above, or under it, but through it. My intent is not to sit on it and feel sorry for myself, blame someone, but to surrender it so that it doesn't keep circling back in bigger ways. Here is an exercise I've used to begin healing pain when it shows up:

1. Label (or acknowledge) the pain (fear, anger, resentment, whatever you're feeling). Notice it and give yourself permission to feel the emotions *without* judgment or trying to get rid of it. This is uncomfortable, but it puts you back in the driver's seat.

2. Ask yourself what gift or lesson might be hidden in this experience. Don't overthink it; this is a starting point to opening up the conversation with yourself. (Sometimes, you don't get an immediate answer and that's okay.)

3. Decide who you need to forgive in this situation (yourself or someone else).

4. Write down one small thing you can do that can help you heal from this. (Sometimes it's praying, or identifying a specific action.)

5. Now it's time to do that one thing. (Yes, do it now.)

The key is to allow yourself to process the emotions of the pain, so you can surrender it. The problem lies when our pain becomes trapped. It creates resistance and starts manifesting in negative ways.

A Lesson on Seeking Clarity

When you *only* view obstacles as obstacles, you won't recognize opportunities when they come. However, when you leverage your obstacles and use them as stepping stones—they will lead you to clarity, growth and fulfillment.

This truth reminds me of a story about Keith Davison, a 94-year-old widower from Morris, Minnesota. Rather than getting stuck in grief after he lost his wife of 66 years to cancer, he installed a pool in his backyard for the neighborhood kids to swim. While his neighbors thought he was a little crazy, he followed through on his plan and not only invited the neighborhood kids and their families to swim, he also took pleasure in enjoying the pool himself.

"I'm not sitting by myself looking at the walls," he told his local news station. Keith was someone who got clear about his story—not one of the past, but one of the future. He could have isolated himself after suffering such a great loss, and understandably so, but that may have shortened his own life. Researchers call this the "widowhood effect," and according to Harvard University sociologists, men are 22% more likely to die shortly after the death of a spouse. Keith Davidson chose to not let his grief write his story. He gave himself permission to change it.

What about you? Will you allow yourself to explore and discover things about your life that haven't been uncovered yet? What are the things that make you unique? What gives you purpose? What makes you cry and laugh? What moves you to make a difference in the world?

What Is Your "Why?"

People have an innate desire to know their purpose and reason for living. This is a foundational question that points us to greater fulfillment and impact we have on others.

In Simon Sinek's book *Start with Why: How Great Leaders Inspire Everyone to Take Action,* he teaches that while it's important for others to know what you do and how you do it, what they really connect with is why you do it (i.e., your purpose) [5]. And I personally saw the evidence: There were people around me that were super clear on their purpose and could articulate it, and they were quite successful.

And then there was me. My "why" eluded me. What was my purpose? To add to it, my perfectionist side would ask, "What if I pick the wrong purpose?"

For me, it was more like a giant jigsaw puzzle with several thousand pieces, and not knowing where the pieces fit.

It can be discouraging if you've struggled with knowing what your exact purpose in life is. Here are some things I wish I knew earlier in the process of discovering my purpose that may help you too:

- **Clarity doesn't come all at once.** It's not an event; it's a process. It's easy to compare yourself to those who seem to have greater clarity, but don't get distracted by someone else's journey. You don't know what it took for them to get to where they are. Instead, focus on the step you're on, then take the next step when it appears (or create the next step if you don't see one). You will get clarity *as* you take action. Don't rush your journey— honor it, knowing that it's shaping who you're becoming, even the uncomfortable parts.

- **Your purpose is not outside you, it's IN you and it's pursuing you.** You just might not recognize it yet. It requires you going deep, but not all at once. As you find out things about yourself, you'll discover attitudes and behaviors that may need a little cleaning up. This is where you develop and test your persistence and commitment to living boldly.

- **Your purpose is unique to YOU.** While I believe we can help people in many ways, we're not meant to help everyone. There is something so unique about you that others that need, and only you can offer it to them in the way that you do.

- **You don't have to know your exact purpose to live a meaningful life.** If you can't articulate what your purpose is, it's okay! You can start by finding out the needs of those around you and how you can use your strengths to help them.

- **Your purpose will bring you joy!** When you find yourself doing things or helping others and you feel lighter and happier, you are living in your purpose. Reflect on what you're doing and how you're specifically doing it, including who you are with and where you are.

Questions About Purpose

Carl Jung said, "Your vision will become clear only when you look into your heart. Who looks outside, dreams. Who looks inside, awakens."

Here are some reflective questions to help you start digging into what your purpose is and what you are passionate about:

- Do you like what you're doing now in this stage of life? What about it do you like or dislike?

- Do you believe in what you're doing?

- How is what you are doing benefiting others?

- What moves you and stirs your heart?

- What reoccurring dreams or ideas have come up in your life that seemed far-fetched, random, or unreachable?

- What have you been told that you are good at over the years, even if you think it's not a big deal?

- Even if you don't have the whole picture, what ARE you clear on?

- What difficult experiences in your life have changed you and what valuable life lessons did you learn from them?

Once you write these out, you'll begin to see common themes and patterns. A great way to go through this is to have someone else write notes while you're sharing your answers and have them identify patterns they see.

A helpful resource to help you narrow down and create a purpose statement or tagline is a book entitled *Find Your Why: A Practical Guide for Discovering Purpose for You and Your Team,* also written by Simon Sinek [6]. My "why" is to inspire people to live boldly and understand the value they bring so they can create more good in the world. I review and tweak this every few months as I still continue to get clarity as I grow.

•••

There is great freedom in pushing past these obstacles of fear, guilt, self-doubt, numbness, and the inability to dream. Which ones do you struggle with the most? Once you start pushing past the limitations of your past, you are already on your way to gaining more clarity and momentum in your life! At times, this will require you to give up comfort—if you remember, my mom left her town, her family, and the only life she knew, and this was where she found freedom. Learning how to push past certain obstacles may be hard, and there will be times you feel like giving up. Don't. As you keep giving yourself permission to become the person you were created to be, you will be able to:

- Help yourself and others more

- Build greater confidence

- See and create opportunities

- Overcome fears

- Uncover your blind spots

- Find peace

- Have greater resilience

Takeaways

- **You are not your past.** How you were raised does not have to define you.

- **You can change the narrative.** By revisiting the past, you can rewrite the story.

- **Learn from what scares you.** Fear can paralyze you or it can motivate you. Learn to see fear as a teacher.

- **Don't take the guilt trip.** Don't take responsibility for the choices of others. They must take responsibility for themselves.

- **Feel the pain to get to the purpose.** Numbing out pain only prevents you from reaching your potential. Learn to confront the pain and push past it.

- **Are you clear?** As you begin to see new possibilities for your life, you'll also find that dreams and goals that once were hazy are now becoming clear.

- **Get to "why."** Your mission in life is unique to you. Only you can discover what it is.

Dig Deeper

- Do you sometimes struggle with fear, doubt, or guilt? Describe when it shows up for you.

- What do you think your purpose on this planet is?

- What three old habits do you need to release to live into your purpose?

- What three new habits do you need to begin?

Chapter 4
Think Different

Create new thought patterns to shift your results

The greater the struggle,
the more glorious the triumph.

— Nick Vujicic

Have you heard of the Australian evangelist and motivational speaker Nick Vujicic? Nick was born with tetra-amelia syndrome, a rare disorder characterized by the absence of arms and legs. Talk about limitations! But Nick didn't allow it to limit him. He found a way to walk, run, swim, and even drive [1].

Nick has been a great source of inspiration for me not only because he has some obvious challenges, but because he "gets" it. He knows what it's like to face real challenges, fears, and yet rise above them.

I first met Nick at a leadership conference that I attend twice a year. He did some training with our team of international trainers and spoke about how he overcame his challenges to building his speaking career. While I was listening to him share his story, I remember initially thinking, *"Wow. How is he so positive with the challenges he faces every day?"* But his mindset, faith, confidence, and energy make you quickly forget that he has no arms and legs.

He's such an engaging storyteller as well as a great teacher. He shared that the limits we believe to be real can limit us only if we allow them to. His words spoke to my heart. That's the mindset I want to remember, especially when I get discouraged.

Until a few years ago, much of what I'd believed were limits in my life were actually perceived and not real. They were limits because I believed them to limit me. When you look at Nick, you probably think, *"He has limits—he has no arms and legs!"* Yes, the lack of limbs creates what many would call massive limitations. But who says it has to keep him from doing things he wants to accomplish in life?

He can and has been able to accomplish many things - drive a car, swim, run, jump, play golf, be a world-renowned speaker, he owns several organizations, he's married and has 4 children! He has learned to do many things, he just does them differently and has lots of help doing them. Nick has trained his mind to look for opportunities despite his challenges—but he wouldn't see them if he used his previous way of thinking. He had to start thinking differently.

My husband and I had the honor of spending a day with Nick at a technology conference held in Santa Clara, California. We had been collaborating with some of the biggest pioneers in virtual reality: how it is being used in a positive way to help people with physical, emotional and medical needs. Nick was the keynote speaker and shared his story with hundreds of people in the entertainment and gaming industry. His call to action was for them to use their gifts and talents to help people with physical disabilities.

Later that day, several of us accompanied Nick in an enormous exhibit hall where technology companies displayed their latest inventions for people to test, most of which were games. I could hardly keep up with him as he sped around on his little scooter (almost running people over!). He was like a kid in a candy store going from booth to booth.

One particular display that caught his eye was a virtual golf course. Before I knew it, Nick lowered his seat down to the ground, jumped onto the artificial turf, and asked the guy at the booth to help him hold the golf club with his neck. The guy, trying not to show his disbelief, helped him put on the virtual reality helmet and Nick took it from there.

Needless to say, he was in his element and he putted away. He drew quite a crowd. People were in awe and inspired by what they were witnessing. He was actually quite good!

While Nick has many extraordinary stories, he is also realistic about what he can and cannot do on his own. He needs help every day for very basic needs—as you can imagine, there is a lot that he can't do independently. But if he wants it bad enough—he doesn't allow it to limit him. He finds a way!

What about you? Are there things that you are allowing to limit you just because you don't know how to do them, or you feel you have a weakness? Think further. Are there things you wanted to do in your past but you didn't believe you could, or someone discouraged you from doing them?

To grasp some of the areas that might be holding you back, consider the following questions:

- What limitation or challenge do you face today?

- Is this limitation real or something you've perceived or believed to be a limit?

- Did someone place this limitation on you or label you?

- What does the limitation prevent you from having in your life?

- How can you start thinking differently so you are more open to trying new things, even if at first they seem too difficult or unattainable?

There are other limits besides having no arms or legs that can have as much of an impact in your life. Maybe your limitation isn't physical. Maybe it's a fear, or a learning challenge; maybe you feel misunderstood or have had some naysayers in your life that didn't support your dreams.

While these all can be challenging, if we don't open ourselves up to thinking differently about them, we miss out on a lot! Could it be that whatever challenge you face might actually have an opportunity embedded in it?

If we give ourselves permission to think in a different way, and tell ourselves our real story, then a challenge becomes a mechanism to uncover a new opportunity, a new hope and quite possibly a new strength that we didn't know we had. The key is to see things differently by thinking differently.

If we aren't open to learning and thinking differently, we aren't growing. If we aren't growing, this will lead to internal stagnation. It's a lot like water. Water is meant to circulate, to move. However, if it stays motionless and stagnant, the water becomes stinky-smelly and life cannot thrive. We are the same way. For the water to become something good it needs some heat, it needs some minerals, and it needs to be stirred.

For us, the heat represents the challenges, the minerals represent the available resources, and the process of stirring represents the different ways to pursue our opportunities. These steps to thinking different are identified in Figure 4.

THINK DIFFERENT

Figure 4 – The Steps to Thinking Different

Look for Challenges

Our challenges can help us discover more inside us. I'm not trying to downplay anything you've gone through. Pain and suffering are real. But they aren't the only thing and we don't have to be miserable while going through them. I've heard it said, "Pain is inevitable, but misery is optional".

In the previous chapter, I shared how it's healthy to acknowledge your emotions so that you can release them, but when you've been stuck in your pain too long, you can easily forget there is more to the picture. However, when we can step back, we see there are truly good things happening in our life simultaneously. That awareness isn't automatic; we must first reshape our thinking.

In one of the youth leadership programs that Nick developed, which I help facilitate in schools, he shares the story of how he used to play soccer as a child (note: he has a tiny little foot that sticks out of his hip that is perfect for kicking). Well, one day he hurt his only foot during school and had to stay in bed until he recovered.

He said it was the worst time of his life. All he could do was stare at the ceiling. He wondered, *"Now what do I have to live for?"* It wasn't until he was faced with the challenge of not being able to move at all that he realized he still had a choice—he could either be angry with God and give up on life (which at one point he almost did), or he could change his outlook on the situation.

He decided that he would stop feeling sorry for himself and find a way to enjoy life more. He discovered things he was good at and started making the right kinds of friends. That injury became a critical turning point for Nick.

Today, Nick leads and inspires millions of people around the world. He shares the message that God loves us and has a purpose for everyone, no matter who we are, what we've done, or what we've been through. Even if it looks like you have limits surrounding you, you can choose to find one thing that is good and focus and build on that one thing until you find other things. If you remain open to learning how to think differently, you discover a more positive attitude and your world opens up to new resources.

Look for Resources

In the book *The Soul of Money: Reclaiming the Wealth of Our Inner Resources,* author Lynne Twist recounts when she was requested to help a tribe in the Sahara Desert with an urgent need— their water supply would soon run out and they had no other resource for water [2].

To compound the problem, the village leaders didn't want outside help as they lived very primitively and didn't want to be influenced by or depend on modern culture, even for water. Lynne, however, probed further. She discovered that the hardworking tribal women had a strong intuition that there was a supply of water under a particular part of the desert not too far away, and that if they dug a well, they would tap into that source.

The men were not open to the idea, as women were not allowed to have a voice in any decisions of the tribe. Nevertheless, Lynne negotiated for the women. Finally, the men begrudgingly agreed that if the women were willing to dig the well, they would allow it.

Over the next few months, the women were allowed to dig holes with borrowed equipment and assisted labor from the government, and lo and behold, they found water. But not just a little amount of water, they discovered a big underground lake. It was the exact resource they needed to keep their village intact so they could still live independently!

Lynne's story is a reminder that when we think we have no resources, a simple change of perspective, getting a little more creative, or listening to the wisdom of others can make all the difference. Often these resources are right in front of us, but we won't ever know unless we're open to seeing what's there.

Look for Other Ways

Your Story, the real one that you long to tell, is a combination of triumphs and struggles, including the missteps. It's a process of learning, unlearning, discovering, and trusting that you are on the right path, even if everything is screaming that you're not. We can learn to use the unpleasant parts of our journey as steps that lead us to discover more.

Often, we create disempowering stories about the parts of our life we don't like. While there might be elements of truth about them, we tend to color the facts with misconstrued feelings that paint an incomplete picture. We crave for our lives to be "normal." My good friend Chris Stapleton reminds me often that normal is a myth and that the real disability is thinking there is only one way of doing things.

Nick's initial story was, "Man, I have no arms and legs. What do I have to offer people? How is my life going to be valuable?" Only when he realized that he could change his story did things change for him. The same can be true for you too!

If you find yourself getting stuck and not seeing past your own challenges, or maybe you've set low goals for yourself because you don't believe you have the ability to reach higher, I encourage you to not settle. Talk to people who have gone through challenges and see how they started thinking differently and how it changed their results. Ask them what their fears and turning points were. I think you'll be surprised that what they did is no great secret; they just figured out another way to see things differently and find the resources they needed.

There have been times in my life when I've become easily discouraged over challenges and became stuck in the same old thought patterns. Sometimes I succumbed to my pity parties, other times I dusted off my knees and started over. Thankfully, we always have the choice to change our thoughts and look for new ways to reach our goals. This can help you see the good even in the most difficult challenges.

A Lesson from Raising My Son

One of my sons struggled in school, especially in certain environments. Often, he would not be able to complete a task, or he would not understand a concept being taught and his anxiety would escalate. He fell further and further behind, even though he was noticeably gifted in several areas.

Watching your child's grades and overall development drop was concerning. We knew it wasn't reflective of his abilities, but we weren't quite sure what the underlying issue was and every year his learning gap got a little bigger.

I decided to homeschool my son for a period of time to see if it would help. At first, I was terrified to teach him. I remember the conversation I had with myself and with my husband. "I don't have a teaching degree. I struggled with school myself, who am I to teach him? What if I ruin his chances of getting into college?"

Eventually I decided to let go of that story and change it. The new one went more like this: "You know, I may not be the smartest person, but even teachers with all the credentials, in our public and private school, have not figured out how to help him. It may take us longer and it may be harder, but we can figure it out. Besides, I have lots of people who can help and I don't have to do this alone."

See how much more empowering that feels? It's not a "Pollyanna" positive pitch, but it leaves room for more possibility. That year of homeschooling him was not easy, but we figured things out. I learned how to create a better learning environment for him; I let him go at his own pace and figured out his learning style so I could adjust the way I taught.

By the end of the year, he was completely caught up and excelled in several of his classes! Had I not changed my story from "who am I to teach my son" to "who am I NOT to teach him," I would have limited myself and in turn limited my son's opportunities.

Good Timber

Here's a portion of a poem I read that shifted my thinking on challenges and weaknesses [3]:

Good timber does not grow with ease:
The stronger wind, the stronger trees;
The further sky, the greater length;
The more the storm, the more the strength.
By sun and cold, by rain and snow,
In trees and men good timbers grow.

— Douglas Malloch
(from *"Good Timber"*)

These words piqued my curiosity and I decided to find out if it was actually true that trees became stronger with wind [4]. This is what I found: In the early 1990s, the University of Arizona created an ecosystem called Biosphere 2 to show how life can support itself in an area as little as three acres.

One of the discoveries they made over a two-year period was the important role that wind played on trees. In this controlled ecosystem, there was no wind. They found that while the trees grew faster, they did not mature well, and once they reached a certain height, they fell over. The reason? Wind strengthens trees by causing them to grow stress wood (which creates resilience) and helps them develop a stronger trunk *and* deeper roots [5].

Without the wind, the tree may appear to be tall and strong, but if too weak on the inside, it would be unable to withstand challenges that are vital to its long-term survival. Whenever you face any challenge, temporarily or over the long haul, remind yourself that inner strength will help you withstand any storm, as long as you allow it to.

So next time you face challenges, remember this story:

Good timber does not grow with ease:
The stronger wind, the stronger trees.

If you're like me, you need frequent reminders because when you're in the middle of a difficult season, you tend to forget what you've already come through. Let those words in the above poem be the seedling that changes your story going forward and allow them to help you start thinking differently.

Having challenges doesn't mean that we are weak; it means we're human and have something in common with every person on the planet. Even the most seemingly perfect people have weaknesses and challenges. I used to be ashamed of my weaknesses.

I'm so grateful that I was wrong and discovered that my biggest weakness was my inability to see my value and my strengths. When we discover the strengths that we do have and then share them with others, life becomes more meaningful.

You are a whole person with your strengths and weaknesses combined. Learn to love all the parts of yourself. At times our weaknesses can lead us to our strengths; it's happened for me, for Nick, and it can happen for you too!

Remember the tree? It needs to weather the challenges in order to learn how to thrive. Yes, it needs lots of sunshine, but it also needs to endure difficult environments. If it grows in a combination of conditions, it can stand the test of time.

Give yourself permission to be bold enough to think differently and live life with a "no limits" kind of mindset like Nick does. Decide to recommit to discovering your strengths despite what you think you lack. It's only when you decide to let your challenges strengthen you that you discover how strong you really are!

Takeaways

- **You are NOT your challenges.** Challenges happen, but they do not define who you are unless you allow them to.

- **See the opportunities.** They are the reward of facing challenges. Learn to identify opportunities in your struggle instead of focusing on the problems.

- **Be resourceful.** Ask yourself better questions to get better answers, and reach out for help. You may not have the answer to change your situation today, but by asking yourself what resources you have available and then taking action, you'll gain access to more ideas and solutions.

- **See yourself differently.** Learn to love yourself and see the beauty of how you are created to seek and live with purpose.

- **Change your story.** Just because it's in the past doesn't mean the story has to stay the same. You can rewrite your story in a way that gives you power, hope, and a brighter future.

- **You are enough!** Learn to change "Woe is me!" into "Why not me?" You can save not only yourself, but others too.

- **Be good timber.** Like trees, you can grow stronger and rise taller than the challenges you face.

Dig Deeper

- What past challenge have you gone through where you came out stronger?

- What can you use from this past challenge that can help you with a current one?

- What part of your current story do you need to rewrite that will help you begin to see things differently?

Chapter 5
Stand Up

Stand tall and don't apologize

*Let your light shine brightly so others can find
their way out of the dark.*

— Unknown

Have you ever heard of "Tall Poppy Syndrome?" It's a pattern of behavior often imposed on others who stand out or who might be growing faster than others. Originally, it applied to people who, in the eyes of society, were becoming successful or prominent. Because of a desire to maintain control, the government in those cultures would "cut them" down to the same level as everyone else [1]. They feared someone getting too powerful, therefore they would lower their status by imposing restrictions.

Sadly, "Tall Poppy Syndrome" still exists today, and while the government does not necessarily enforce it, those around us sometimes initiate it. In our generation, it's applied to people who want to grow way beyond their current situation, and in doing so they often become successful and stand out. When someone takes a new direction and experiences success, those around them might naturally be uncomfortable, and in some cases resent those who are advancing further than they are.

This syndrome is named after the poppy, which is a striking flower that grows tall and straight. Most poppy fields, which are

65

prominent in Europe, are all about the same height. But what you might not know is that poppies that grow taller than the rest are often cut down and limited to the height of the others. If they grow too tall, they are simply trimmed back. Hence the name "Tall Poppy Syndrome".

In an interview with *People* magazine, Naomi Watts, an English actress and film producer, shared the affects this had on her during her early acting career. She described how some of her friends didn't understand or became jealous of her success and would make passive aggressive comments that caused her to question her dreams and abilities. In describing the syndrome, she remarked, "The poppies grow together, and they're supposed to be uniform. If one grows up too high, it means it's got to be slashed and cut back down to size. People don't like it if you succeed too much. It makes them feel bad."

Have you also experienced this in your life? It can show up in different ways. Perhaps people questioned you when you went outside your comfort zone and started experiencing growth, or you became a much happier person. Have you held yourself back in fear that someone would question you, or that they might feel inferior if you shined a little brighter? The intent of "Tall Poppy Syndrome" is to make everyone the same, to level the playing field, but the impact is that no one strives to get better or pursue the unique greatness that is inside each of them.

As for me, it's interesting how "Tall Poppy Syndrome" played out in my life. Ironically, I've always been tall, and physically stood out above the other kids. After elementary school, I became a wallflower. I did everything I could to *keep from* standing out. But it was kind of impossible not to stand out when you are the tallest kid in your class. On top of that, I was skinny. I had nicknames like "beanpole," "barbwire," "noodle," and "Olive Oyl" (yes, from the cartoon *Popeye*).

I can laugh today, but back then those comments more than stung. I stood out in ways I didn't want to. I wanted to feel normal and fit in. Even though some of these comments were done in fun, I took them personally and used it as evidence that I didn't fit in, and in turn cut myself down.

When I would occasionally come out of my shell, I worked hard to stay out. Years later, when I started living more boldly, I decided to pursue my career as a certified coach and speaker. While there were some who were excited for me and encouraged me, there were a few people who were uncomfortable with the changes I was making. Whenever I was around them, I found myself reverting back to my "wallflower" days.

When you start taking a stand for your life, sometimes there will be those who don't support you and times you will stand alone. *When* that happens, keep standing tall. Your initial reaction may be to shrink back to your old size, but we aren't meant to grow backward. Find others who fully support you, and believe in you, and encourage your growth.

There's a part of us that wants to fit in so we can feel accepted by others. Yet the brutal truth is we were never meant to fit in. We were meant to shine and connect with others in all our unique and glorious ways. "Fitting in" and "connecting with others" are not the same. When we truly connect, we accept each other for our differences without expecting each other to change. We celebrate our individual gifts by allowing the other person to be themselves, even if it's very different from who we are.

Sometimes a relationship can dissolve if someone isn't willing to accept you for who you are and who you are becoming. I've become accustomed to the reality that sometimes others aren't going to like my boldness and that's okay. We need to decide whether we will shrink back, or stay true to who we are. As illustrated in Figure 5, I found five essentials to standing up that help me in my relationships.

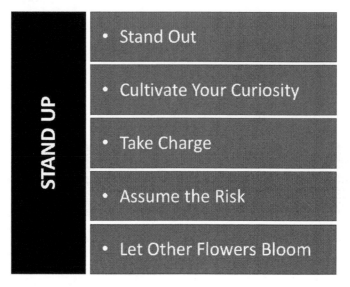

Figure 5 – The Essentials to Standing Up

Stand Out

The first essential to standing up is be willing to stand out. Yes, it is risky and uncomfortable. It requires giving ourselves permission—to make mistakes and be okay with being awkward when trying something new for the first, second and third time. I learned this when I found the courage to put myself in more social situations, which was completely uncomfortable at first. I knew if I was going to move past my fears, I needed to face them.

Too often we want to fit in and belong. But in trying to fit in, we hide who we are and get only a temporary feeling of belonging. Being willing to stand out gives us a voice. It empowers us to speak up for ourselves, express our truth, and share our ideas and opinions.

It empowers us to be comfortable in our skin regardless of what's happening around us or who is in the room.

Do you remember the song "The Hokey Pokey?" As a young girl, I would go to the roller-skating rink (another socially awkward place for me), and we'd gather to the middle of the rink and the song would begin:

"You put your left foot in,
you put your left foot out..."

If you didn't follow the directions in the song, you were out. A lot like "Mother May I?" you had to always follow the rules, or you were out of the game. While fun and innocent, it's another example how we can play our own internal game of getting stuck in patterns. We are either asking for permission ("Mother May I?") or we are following the crowd ("The Hokey Pokey"). If we truly want to live more fully, we have to recognize, and interrupt old patterns and replace them with new ones.

Cultivate Your Curiosity

Interrupting patterns begins with a mindset of openness and curiosity. Back when I was wondering what was wrong with me and why I wasn't fitting in, I was still very curious. That curiosity was an important tool for eventual breakthrough.

A common way people cope with pain is to stay busy. And that's how I initially dealt with my pain. I became a performance-based, Type A perfectionist. It wasn't until I began to get curious and ask myself questions, that I began to find answers I already had inside me.

Giving yourself permission to get curious can be a game changer. You may not initially like what you see, but there's still more to be found. Be open. First, notice and recognize how far you've come. From where you started to where you are now has been a process. There are old patterns to shed and belief systems to disrupt, so don't focus on how much catching up you have to do or you'll easily get discouraged. Know that you are exactly where you need to be to figure out the next step.

I started digging deep into my old patterns about seven years ago. Like me, you may likely come to the realization that much of what you've been thinking has limited you. Those beliefs can be hard to shake off. Just recognize even though you may be a work in progress, it's *progress* as long as you stay curious!

The process of changing old beliefs can at times be a messy business. Rather than putting more effort and time into something that hasn't worked, instead focus your energy on what you want and what has worked in the past. Move away from thinking about your limitations and start thinking about your opportunities—even the ones you can't see yet.

We're prone to be creatures of habit, but if we want to stand out and live boldly, we need to reexamine what we do and why we do it. When the seed of curiosity is allowed to grow, our best selves will learn to shine. It's at that point we can move away from the limited, "cut back" version of ourselves and learn to stand tall.

Take Charge

I met a young lady, Paige, who shared the following experience after graduating from college. Paige was eager to begin her life in the real world and landed a promising job at a highly touted recruiting firm. However, what began as excitement grew into extreme frustration. The environment was cutthroat and she didn't realize she would be competing with everyone else on her team.

You see, despite being a team, each person was contending to recruit and fill the same jobs in the marketplace. And employees didn't get compensated unless they met their goals. Despite being encouraged to work as a team, every time Paige would ask for help, people would withhold information for fear of giving away their "secret sauce" of filling positions. And whenever Paige reached her goals and shared her ideas, the team would "knock her down a peg" and dismiss anything she suggested.

Quickly, Paige began to question herself and her abilities but kept forging ahead because she was determined to succeed. She felt she had to prove that she was a good recruiter and that she had what it took even if she didn't get the support she needed, but it didn't come without a price.

Her life took an unexpected turn when her mother noticed Paige wasn't her cheerful self and was no longer full of energy. After seeing a doctor, Paige was diagnosed with anxiety and depression. She was on a downward spiral and it was having an emotional and physical impact on her. With her mom's help, Paige began to realize that she had not been in an environment where she could flourish. At work, she had no one to support or encourage her. They were only interested in meeting their goals at any cost, even if that meant cutting each other down—another classic example of "Tall Poppy Syndrome."

Thankfully, Paige took charge and quit her job. Over the next few months, she got her health back on track and focused on things that brought her meaning in life. When she was able to go back to work, she went into a completely different career that focused on helping support small businesses. Today, Paige lives a life where she pursues her curiosity once again, and because of that, she is no longer allowing herself to be "cut back" by others. Her story is a reminder that you can come back even when others cut you down. The key is to get curious and take charge!

Why People Fear Standing Out

Learning a new skill, reaching new goals, or stepping into something different can sometimes create tension with those around us, even in our relationships. And when we just want to do our best, and others judge or sabotage us, it can hurt and leave us feeling emotionally abandoned. In some cases, people become envious of what we've created or they're uncomfortable because it reminds them of actions they haven't taken in their own lives.

If you're growing in any kind of way, you will automatically stand out, whether you want to or not. People will notice you're different and not in the same place. When you have people that want to cut you down to their level, they aren't interested in supporting your growth; they would rather commiserate than celebrate with you. Commiserating can create a false sense of bonding and belonging, but it's not authentic and doesn't last. Sadly, most people choose the lesser version of themselves because their desire to have a sense of belonging is a stronger pull than their sense of being.

But once you recognize that standing out is one of the sacrifices of growing, you can learn to accept this and move on. It becomes much easier to work through disappointments, even when others don't believe in you, because your belief in yourself has taken root. And if people try to talk you into going back to your old self, you will find yourself resilient against the old pull of choosing belonging over being.

You can learn to stand tall and guilt-free. When you do, look for the people that come into your path that DO believe in you and encourage you to keep growing. When you discover these people, keep them close!

Assume the Risk

Some of the first risks we took were as babies when we began to crawl. We weren't conscious of the dangers, though our parents were always there to catch us or steer us in safe directions, and we kept on going. We'd see that toy car across the room, and that object became our one and only goal. We focused on it until we reached it. We didn't let anything stop us, and sometimes resorted to throwing a tantrum until someone retrieved it for us.

As adults, we get into our real cars to go to work, with distracted drivers all around us. We often don't even think about the risks we put ourselves in daily. Some risks are low and we have more control over them, and some are high.

When it comes to our identity and how we see ourselves, we also become aware of how others view us and how they respond to our and ambition and goals. We create big goals, then we fear taking the necessary risks to reach them. Our willingness or unwillingness to take those risks becomes a factor in our pursuit of achieving them. Instead of being locked in on our goal, we become over-focused on outside responses. We start to doubt the outcome, we become scared to make the first move, and if we do move, we only go a certain distance before evaluating the risk again.

When we become fearful of taking risk, we sometimes equate opportunities with danger, even if they will help us achieve what we want. But the real danger is sacrificing our growth for 'easy'. It's when we settle for a life of doing the bare minimum, and not giving life to our dreams, we starve the person we're capable of becoming.

What if instead of seeing our goals and dreams as dangerous risks, we see them as the start of a new adventure? The more steps you take, the more comfortable you'll feel taking the next step and the one after that. It creates a new pattern and over time the voice of fear loses its power.

Once you taste significance and adventure in your life, you'll develop a different relationship with risk. You'll see the positive impact it can have on others and you'll be open to the possibilities that await you when you stand up and act.

That doesn't mean fear goes away completely, but by allowing yourself to be uncomfortable, knowing you're working towards a greater goal, you'll be more committed to pushing through the temporary discomfort. This way of thinking, even if it initially feels counter-productive, nourishes your natural curiosity, which we were all born with. Yet, we were told as we got older that "It's better to be safe than sorry." Here's why doing what feels "safe" can actually be internally harmful:

- It keeps you in your comfort zone, so you can't grow.

- It shelters you from facing your fears by casting doubt into your mind (e.g., the "What if's…").

- It prevents you from finding your purpose, leaving you to live other people's dreams for your life.

- It quiets your voice, preventing you from sharing your message with the world.

- It keeps you from shining your unique light.

Remember, no risk, no reward. The key to standing up is to assume and embrace the risk.

From Fear to Freedom

When I started facing my fears, my goal was to eliminate them all. I wanted them over and done with. In attempting so, I realized another dilemma: My expectations were way too high, and as a result my fear compounded. It wasn't until I changed my goal from "elimination" of fear to simply experiencing "less" fear that I took the pressure off myself. I changed my all-or-nothing approach to a "less is more" thought process. When fears surface now, I remind myself how far I've come, and then I shift my focus to helping others, which in turn quiets my fear.

Let Other Flowers Bloom

Lifting one another up and encouraging each other is also important for our growth. It can change your perspective from "me" centric to "we" centric—and it frees us from thinking we have to compete with each other.

Give yourself permission to shine and encourage others to shine their light too. Start with remembering that others also have fear, and that others have a need for belonging. Recognize that many of them are being "cut back" too—just like you have been. But you can change the cycle just by your encouragement.

The following words written by Marianne Williamson [2] powerfully remind us that shining our light isn't just for our benefit.

Our deepest fear is not that we are
inadequate. Our deepest fear is that we are
powerful beyond measure.
It's our light, not our darkness,
that most frightens us.
We ask ourselves, who am I to be brilliant,
gorgeous, talented, fabulous?
Actually, who are you not to be?
You're a child of God. You're playing small.
Playing small doesn't serve the world.
There's nothing enlightened about shrinking

so other people won't feel insecure around you.
We are all meant to shine, as children do.
We are born to make manifest the glory of God
that's within us.
It's not just in some of us. It's in everyone.
And as we shine our own light,
we unconsciously give other people permission
to do the same.
As we are liberated from our own fear,
our presence automatically liberates others.

— Marianne Williamson

As you shine your light, remember you don't need other people's permission to grow and enjoy life to the fullest. You make the rules. Be curious. Be encouraging. Be you! As you shine your light, give other people permission to do the same. You'll find that this is an essential to building your own confidence in standing up.

A Lesson from a Guided Missile

The journey toward living boldly works a lot like guided missile. In my government contracting career, I worked as a financial analyst for a missile program. I learned when missiles are shipped, they don't just ship the whole missile, but in pieces including the warhead, target detector, fin, rocket motor, and everything that holds it together. Once the pieces reach the final destination, the missile is *then* assembled like a giant-size LEGO kit (only it takes much longer). Life is the same way. It comes in pieces, and it takes some time.

Guided missiles also come with guidance control software, which processes the information and calculates the proper course for the missile. This software, which is always running in the background, can be likened to a plane's cruise control, which keeps a plane on track by calculating its course.

As for a missile and a plane, it doesn't just go from point A to point B in a straight line. There's a constant series of positive and negative shifts that keep it on course. This means that despite being essentially off course, it still gets to where it's programmed to go because it's always course correcting.

The same is true for how our brain works when we give it a clear, targeted goal. Sometimes we get off course and have to make small adjustments, but those shifts are a necessary important part of the process. Sometimes our course correction comes in the form of examining and changing our limiting thoughts or making mistakes.

Failure to recognize these shifts are a normal part of goal achievement, can cause us to doubt our goals and ourselves. Sometimes we think we're going in the wrong direction, so we stop before we even reach our target. But getting *off* course is necessary for success.

That's the human element too. Like a guided missile, you and I also have inner guidance. For me, that inner guidance comes from a source that I recognize as God. You may recognize it as something else. But when we trust that inner guidance and stand up and start acting, even when we get off track, we can trust and have faith that we're going to course correct. When you live by that faith, fear and risk fall back and your growth begins to skyrocket.

Takeaways

- **Cultivate your curiosity.** Get curious about when you feel most alive and what holds you back from stepping out. Be open, call out those limiting beliefs, and explore how you can change them into more empowering words.

- **Stand out.** Don't be afraid to grow and share your progress with others. If they are not comfortable, that has more to do with where they are than where you are.

- **Break from comfort.** It's easy to go with the flow. If you want to live your bold life, you have to be willing to stretch out of your comfort zone and try new things.

- **Take a risk.** Challenge your beliefs. Every day you take risks unconsciously. Be cognizant of the risks you need to take to reach your goals and stand apart. Big risk, big reward.

- **Guide your achievement missile.** Set a course and remember, missiles don't fly in a straight line. You're going course correct along the way.

Dig Deeper

- When has someone limited you or cut you down when you wanted to grow and change?

- Do you sometimes hold back or cut yourself down? If so, in what specific situations?

- If you were to take one small action step to move forward, despite the discomfort, what would it be?

Chapter 6
Grow Slow

Don't rush a masterpiece in process

A mind that is stretched by a new experience can never go back to its old dimensions.

— James Allen

Growth is a necessary part of life. This is obvious when it comes to our physical bodies, our education, and developing skills. It's also necessary for developing our potential and living a life of significant meaning. Sadly, for many people, after they graduate from college, get a job, start raising a family, and take on other responsibilities, their growth slows way down, and for many it stops altogether.

They don't necessarily stop because they want to. Often it becomes too hard and inconvenient with all the other responsibilities they have, and "life" just seems to take over. But growth matters! And how you grow determines how far you will go in your life and how fulfilled you will be. Growth doesn't happen quickly, and I think that's why many people get discouraged. They want it fast, like everything else. It takes time and it's certainly not a sprint.

I remember getting my first hermit crab at seven years old. These funny-looking creatures, walking around with shells on their backs, totally fascinated me. I would always choose the one at the pet store that was too big for his britches, or in this case, shell.

Having one as a pet was fun, but even beyond that, it was on my "bucket list" to witness one change to a bigger shell.

To them I probably looked creepy, as I would sit peeking from behind my chair watching them for hours. Why? I didn't want to miss my chance. Changing shells isn't something they often do in public, which now I totally get! At that time, I just thought they were being modest; I didn't know it was a matter of survival. While their claws and much of their body are like armor, their tail is extremely soft and contains all of their major organs. Lucky for me, I finally saw "it" happen.

It was the coolest thing ever to watch, almost as exciting as Christmas. Over the next few years, I would witness other hermit crabs trading their smaller home for a larger condo. As they continued to grow, staying put wasn't an option; each crab had to be willing to expose himself to move into a new home. Now I know this is just a crab, or a decapod crustacean if you want to get technical about it. But real growth is the same of you and me too. We have to get out of our shell.

When we want to go out and discover who we were created to be, or go after a new opportunity, or even come out of our "shell," it's a process that doesn't happen quickly. It requires a lot of patience. It also involves certain risks, which leaves us feeling vulnerable and exposed.

Often, we want to rush growth and just get "there." I've tried to grow fast, and while progress was made, I missed out on other growth opportunities that only happens when we slow down. I've found there is great value in growing slowly, knowing that when we reach a certain level of growth, it's temporary. We're not meant to stay there.

As I changed my thinking about how quickly growth should be, I first needed to understand certain elements of the growth process. These elements are illustrated in Figure 6.

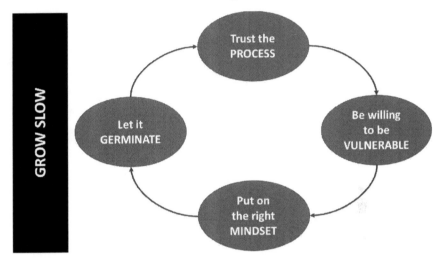

Figure 6 – The Four Elements of Slow Growth

As you read more about these, I hope it will encourage you to get rid of your current "shell" and move on to something new that will expand your whole self!

Element #1 – Trust the Process

Aside from hermit crabs changing the shells on their back, they also molt, which is a process of shedding their skin, (much like a snake or lizard). Molting is stressful on the crab. But it's how it grows. When it leaves its old skin, its soft exterior, even the claws, has to take time to harden. This is double the vulnerability, so during this process they bury themselves in sand for protection and insulation from external elements and predators. Once their outer bodies harden, they can return to their shells where they are safe and sound.

This process parallels our own life. Consider how the vulnerable crab moving between shells or molting is similar to our own growth. When we get out of our comfort zone to move past our fears and towards a larger dream, it can be terrifying, and it can almost feel like we're dying, but it is necessary for our growth and development.

I remember times I've felt vulnerable—I wanted to scurry like the little crab to get to a place where I could hide, feel safe, and be more comfortable. Eventually, I found that when I stayed in my comfort zone too long, I stopped growing completely. This is why playing it 'safe' can be more harmful to your internal growth *than* being BOLD and taking scary steps.

Yes, this can feel terrifying, but it's also where you make new discoveries, access opportunities, and find yourself. The first step in growing into who we want to be is to trust the process, knowing that you are on the right path even if it doesn't feel like it.

When you need to step back and regroup, that is okay! Sometimes we need to get our bearings to prepare for the next step. The danger is in staying still too long. That's when we don't notice the stagnation, or atrophy. We experience it as restlessness and think that by staying in our comfort zone it will provide us what we need to ease that feeling.

But what if we need movement and vulnerability to go to the next level? A part of my process is also trusting that God is always working on my behalf, even if I can't see the big picture yet.

Element #2 – Be Willing to Be Vulnerable

It's in the nature of hermit crabs to protect themselves, but when they do come out of their shells, they emerge in all their naked glory so they can experience growth. Figuratively, we have to be willing to do the same; at times we need to get "naked"—in a transparent, open, and authentic sense. And like a hermit crab, we need to learn the right conditions for when and when not to do this.

For some, the word "vulnerable" tends to only take on a negative meaning, and that we are weak if we let others see a different side of us. But when we are willing to share our struggles, victories, fears, *and* growth with people, even if we expose our flaws, it can lead to greater connection with people, often building or rebuilding trust and strengthening relationships.

But why is being open with others so hard to do? It turns out that when we expose our growth, ideas, and thoughts to others, or find our voice, we sense the risk, and the fear. We believe we *are* more susceptible to criticism, and maybe even rejection from others. Because of that, we want to stay in our shell. We would rather withdrawal from growth.

Take a moment and think about a time you wished you could have been more open, but you hesitated. Or a time you shared something with someone you wished you *hadn't* because it completely backfired. Maybe they disagreed with what you said, or they were completely silent and looked at you like you had a third eye. Or maybe you didn't get the support you wanted.

I can remember a few times I wished I had kept my mouth shut, but yet again, I'm glad I didn't. Those moments stretched me and grew me. Over time it's become easier, and yet sometimes I still struggle with opening up to others. Sharing thoughts, ideas, and even our struggles can be scary, but it can also be freeing when the walls we built around us start to come down. We need to remember that our growth and success is always on the other side of being vulnerable.

"Safe" and "Unsafe" Relationships

I've found that a healthy transparency with people isn't about wearing your heart on your sleeve. It's about using your inner wisdom to know not only what to share but also with whom to share and when.

In *Safe People: How to Find Relationships that are Good for You and Avoid Those That Aren't,* Dr. Henry Cloud and Dr. John Townsend talk about how being vulnerable with toxic people can backfire [1]. An "unsafe" person pushes people down in order to lift themselves up, whether passively or aggressively. If you've experienced any kind of trauma caused by someone else, it can often be a challenge to know which people in your life you can trust.

A "safe" person encourages and supports your growth no matter what. They may not always agree with you, but they always look out for your best interests and believe in you. If you know someone like this, stay close to them; they are your peeps! If you don't know anyone like this, you may have to look around or start changing who you are hanging around with, they are there!

Yes, being vulnerable is risky. We may not always get it right, but in doing so we open ourselves up to being even bolder and creating the change we want. This too is the normal process of growth and eventually it will get easier. But don't get too comfy...you'll soon outgrow that shell too!

In his book *Resilience: Facing Down Rejection and Criticism on the Road to Success,* Mark McGuinness explains how resilience is a test we must pass when we want to play BIG in life [2]. Without it, we'll cave much faster when we make a mistake. We'll lack commitment in following through. When we stay true to ourselves, even in those times when we feel vulnerable, we need to continually say to ourselves, "I am committed to doing this no matter what!"

Are you willing to grow no matter what?

Are you willing to be vulnerable, especially when it's uncomfortable?

It's only when you get of your old shell and prepare for the new that you can experience steady growth.

Element #3 – Put on the Right Mindset

Growth isn't just about process and being vulnerable, it's also about having a healthy mindset to match. This doesn't mean you're always thinking happy thoughts 100% of the time and always have a smile on your face. But it does mean you are committed to seeing things from a perspective that is aligned with your growth.

There are some stories in the Bible that fascinate me. Like when the Pharisees (who in my opinion were just a bunch of busy-bodies) questioned Jesus about fasting. He and his disciples were not participating in the fast that many others were. When questioned, Jesus' response was, "No one sews a patch of unshrunk cloth on an old garment. Otherwise, the new piece will pull away from the old, making the tear worse. And no one pours new wine into old wineskins. Otherwise, the wine will burst the skins, and both the wine and the wineskins will be ruined. No, they pour new wine into new wineskins [3]." *What?*

This is a story I needed to explore a little more, and while I can't be completely sure, this is what I think he was talking about. While Jesus was talking about cloth and wine, I believe he was really speaking about the Pharisees' rigid, and black and white mindset. They had a reputation for upholding tradition and forcing others to follow laws. Kind of controlling, don't you think? This was what Jesus was challenging. He brought about a fresh perspective, a mindset that would usher in a time where people could approach

God based on His grace and the abundant living He could give us, not on fear-based laws. So, really, what does all this have to do with wine and cloth? Let's take this a little further.

Freshly made wine is in a state of fermentation. As gasses expand during this process, a fresh wineskin (made of animal skin) absorbs the expansion and ages with the wine during the process until it's completed.

But if you put fresh wine into an *old* wineskin that has already hardened, you run into a problem. The fermentation process and expansion of gasses will fill the old container and cause it to burst from internal pressure. This burst ruins both the wine and skin.

In the same way, a growth mindset won't "take" in someone who has a completely rigid mindset. A fixed mind can't properly hold or process new information; it's not yet ready. That's why it is important for us to not only develop a mindset that is fertile for growth, but also surround ourselves by others who do too. If you're constantly around people who are close-minded, it will affect and slow down your growth.

Fixed Mindset Versus a Growth Mindset

A fixed or rigid mind is unwilling to bend and is not a nurturing ground for goals or growth. This is why, in your journey of living more boldly, it's helpful to understand your process of thinking and the mindset of those you spend time with. Let's explore this by looking at the contrasts of both of these mindsets.

FIXED MINDSET	GROWTH MINDSET
"This is the way things are and always will be."	"I may not be able to control everything around me, but there are things I can change, and it starts with me."

"This is impossible."	"This may be hard now, but it will eventually get easier if I keep trying."
"I will never have enough money."	"I'm willing to invest in things that help me expand my abilities."
"I don't have time for anything else in my life."	"I make time for the things that are important to me."
"I have to figure things out before I start."	"Once I take that first step, I trust the next step will become more clear."

Notice the differences in these mindsets and attitudes? Which one do you think will promote more sustained growth? In *The 15 Invaluable Laws of Growth: Live Them and Reach Your Potential*, John C. Maxwell shares eight mindset traps that prevent us from taking steps of growth [4].

- **The Assumption Gap:** "I assume I will automatically grow."

- **The Knowledge Gap:** "I don't know how to grow."

- **The Timing Gap:** "It's not the right time to begin."

- **The Mistake Gap:** "I'm afraid of making mistakes."

- **The Perfection Gap:** "I have to find the best way before I start."

- **The Inspiration Gap:** "I don't feel like doing it."

- **The Comparison Gap:** "Others are better than I am."

- **The Expectation Gap:** "I thought it would be easier than this."

Which mindset traps do you sometimes get caught in? Understanding these helped me identify areas in my thinking that were rigid.

Developing a Growth Mindset

Many people think they should be able to go from a fixed mindset to a growth mindset quickly, but get frustrated when they don't see the results. Remember, it's a process that doesn't happen overnight. Start by being open to more growth. This will immediately begin to expand your awareness, eventually leaving little room for your old ways of thinking.

Begin with giving yourself permission to be open to the idea of always learning. If you're not open to it, you're not ready for real growth. If you're not willing to be open to new ways of thinking, but still expect to get better results, then you'll end up frustrated and you'll blame someone or something outside yourself. I've observed this with people who would say they want help, but when it came down to thinking differently, they were unwilling and they continued getting the same unwanted results. You can't put new wine into old wineskins, remember?

Developing a growth mindset comes back to being willing to get curious and ask yourself the difficult questions. Starting with "What has worked in my life so far?" "What is not working?" "Why is that?" "What do I really want?" and "What am I willing to change?"

Questions like these can be hard, but they can also create forward movement. Be open. Asking the right questions can draw out the needed answers.

A Lesson from Macarons

An example of these first three elements of growth is beautifully captured by my friend Andi, who is one of the owners of Agora Downtown Coffee Shop. She developed a passion for making macarons as a pastry offering for her clients. I asked her one day, "What makes your cookies so much better than others I've tasted?" She said with a twinkle in her eye, "Macarons are a fickle little cookie, but they are such a labor of love." My response, of course, was, "Tell me more!"

She went on to share that it took her almost four months to get to the place where she could successfully bake them. Up until that point, two out of three batches failed and there was a lot of lost time and expensive ingredients. But eventually she mastered it. It was a process of experimenting and asking questions: Why were the tops cracking? Why were there inconsistencies? At first it frustrated her and at one point she even felt like giving up, thinking, *"I've never done this before and they're turning out a total flop."* But she stuck with it and made small adjustments. She changed her attitude from "I'll never get this right" to "This is an experiment."

Now she has perfected the recipe and instead of Italian or French-style macarons, she combined the two and created a whole different style of her own. Even French people who have visited her shop say, "Your macaron is the best I've ever tasted."

This wouldn't be possible had she not challenged herself to stick with her process. She told me, "It can actually be a blessing for things *not* to go as planned." Some of her best recipes were unplanned, or as she calls it a "product of desperation." She also learned to trust herself. At first, she had no confidence in her ability because she had never done it before. But eventually she learned she had to trust her gut, and if it didn't work, try something different.

During the time when the batches were failing, she learned to repurpose the failed cookies into something else. As she was sharing all this with me, I was eating one of her cookies that was dipped in chocolate, and she pointed and said, "You know, you're eating one of my failed macarons!" I'm inspired by Andi's willingness to give herself permission to fail, learn, and try again.

Here is Andi's advice for enduring slow and frustrating processes where things don't go as planned and the growth seems too slow.

- **Enjoy the process.** There will be rough spots. Find joy along the way.

- **Make it fun.** When she would think, *"Oh, gosh. I have to make macarons again,"* she would put on some fun music and bake. It made the whole process more enjoyable, whether it resulted in a good or bad batch.

- **Seek info.** Get the skills you need. She asked questions and watched videos. Think of where you can get more information to help you with your process.

- **Don't get caught up in one set of rules.** Keep an open mind. Do things unconventionally. Listen to the professionals, but don't hold yourself to following their rules. Learn to trust yourself.

- **The time is right when the time is right.** When you're eager to grow and it seems like it's taking forever, the perfect time is the time you're in.

Many times, we get a rush out of checking something off our list. In that striving to accomplish a goal, sometimes we end up missing the most important lessons, and even opportunities, because we are going full speed and never slowing down. I've found that lasting joy comes from getting the most out of the process. When we aren't willing to slow down or look at different viewpoints, the goal can become fleeting, and then we find ourselves looking for the next shiny goal.

The little shifts in Andi's mindset helped her to create a whole new style of macaron that people now flock to her store to buy.

Element #4 – Let it Germinate

Like most efforts, we usually see the fruits of our labor and growth *after the fact*. We reflect and see that it was worth the hard work and relish in what we've gained. Like the cookies and macarons that Andi bakes, you have to let things take shape. You can't yank them out of the oven before they're ready. Letting growth take shape requires lots of patience. Farmers understand this more than anyone through the Law of Germination.

The Law of Germination

When a farmer works the land—preparing, plowing the field, and planting the seeds—he knows there's a long time from when the seed is planted to when it will yield a crop. He doesn't expect the food to pop out of the seed without certain things taking place first. He trusts and believes in the process and goes about the rest of his work while he waits for that plant to produce the harvest.

It's the same for us. In our growth and development, there's a long period of time when we won't yet see the fruits of our hard labor. That's when most people quit. But here's the thing: There are things happening inside us that we can't see yet. Each "seed" of growth we plant in ourselves, whether it's a dream, goal or idea, also has a germination period. It takes a lot of persistence, trust, and understanding that what's happening is exactly how it's supposed to take place. The growth of those seeds depends on many factors, including our mindset and environment.

Eventually, the seeds we plant will surface and we'll start seeing results. When that time comes, we'll get excited and think it happened out of nowhere. Yet it's been growing and taking root the whole time, preparing for a harvest. This concept was encouraging to me as it meant I didn't have to wait until I saw the *visible* results to know that growth was occurring. I could celebrate now! And likewise for you, don't wait until you see the results to celebrate your growth; celebrate now and trust that something is at work below the surface and in time you will see the breakthrough!

Sometimes we need to go below the surface and explore the foundation that's being created. Even though this can often be uncomfortable, there is sweet reward ahead (even some unexpected surprises!). When archaeologists dig, they have to go deep to find the treasured artifacts. Often, they dig not knowing what to expect but they know they have to dig if they are to find a treasure. Are you ready to dig? Grab a shovel. Remember the treasure is rarely near the surface. It's often buried deep. But it's there…if you want it.

Neale Donald Walsch said it best: "Everything is falling together perfectly, even though it looks as if some things are falling apart. Trust in the process you are now experiencing."

Your germination period is preparing you for a breakthrough. It's how seeds mature, and roots take hold. If you don't prepare, you won't be rooted. Be willing to learn and fail while the process takes shape.

Takeaways

- **Be vulnerable.** We can stunt our growth when we're too protective and have inner walls up. Look for quality relationships to help you come out of your shell.

- **Discern who is "safe" and who is not.** Not everyone has our best interests in mind. Some people fear change and are afraid of you changing. They may sabotage your progress. Surround yourself with those who will empower you to grow.

- **Go from a fixed mindset to a growth mindset.** You're either growing or you're stagnant. When you have rigid thinking, you can't see or appreciate the surrounding opportunities. When you have a growth mindset, you are open to learning. Identify which one is your default mindset. If it's more fixed, begin the process of opening yourself up to have more of a growth mindset.

- **Keep moving.** It may seem like you aren't growing when you actually are. The Law of Germination states that when a farmer plants a seed, it will grow in its appropriate time. Keep watering your seeds and in time they will grow.

- **Don't rush growth.** We all want to grow, and when we don't grow as fast as expected, we get discouraged and want to quit. Be patient. Growth is a long game, but the evidence shows itself when you stay in it.

- **Embrace the process.** Have fun, make mistakes, and fall in love with the journey. That's where you will do the most growing. Not at the end.

- **Dig deep.** As you grow, don't be afraid of what's below the surface. By asking questions with a fresh perspective, you'll discover the "gold" inside you!

Dig Deeper

- Think of a time when you tried something new and it took a while to master it. What did you learn about yourself?

- Think of a situation now that is taking longer to get through than you would like. What can you use from your previous experiences to help change your perspective about the current one?

- What advice would you give to others who want better results but it is taking much longer than they want?

Chapter 7
Breathe Deep

Being present is your superpower

There are some things you learn best in calm,
and some in storm.

— Willa Cather

It was a beautiful late afternoon in West Palm Beach, the day before a three-day training event for international coaches and trainers. Many of us had been invited to one coach's house to celebrate her mother's recent survival after a bout with cancer.

I'm not a big fan of crowds; to be honest, I avoid them whenever possible. Yet I found myself stuck smack-dab in the middle of close to 150 people in her modest-size great room and pool area. I attempted to distract from my discomfort by being social and small talk, but then things started getting really tight—literally.

I felt my breath get shallow, then started feeling lightheaded and completely trapped, with the sea of people forcing weight on all sides. I tried to create more space around me, but that was a total waste of time. I had never experienced a full-blown panic attack, but there I was, having one in front of everyone, mostly strangers. I started pushing through the crowd toward the front door. People at first thought I was being rude, but then after seeing the look on my face, they quickly paved a way for me, it was as if the Red Sea parted.

As soon as I crossed the threshold, I leapt off the porch onto the lawn heaving. I thought I was dying and had one of those life-flash-before-my-eyes moment. All I could think of was that I wasn't ready to go yet! It was a scary and seemed the more I fought to get control of my breath, the more I couldn't breathe.

Don't Fight It

Out of nowhere, I felt a hand on my back rubbing in a circular motion accompanied with gentle words in a sweet Southern draw, "Don't fight it, sweetie. Just breathe slowly and all the way out. I know it's scary but just ride the wave, even if it's a big one. Just ride it." She repeated those words over and over while rubbing my back.

My first thought was, *"Lady you're nuts! Ride it out?"* Then I asked her with what breath I had, "What do you mean?" She explained that in order to get to the other side where it's calm, I needed to welcome the feeling I was experiencing. To "Go through it!" So, as scary as it was, I did what Chandler said. At first, it felt as if every cell in my body would explode. But soon my breathing started to become more controlled. Within a few minutes, I felt a calmer.

This moment for me was a "storm" experience, and my initial knee-jerk reaction was to escape. Perhaps you've experienced something similar. Maybe not a full-blown panic attack but feeling overwhelmed on all sides, not seeing an end in sight.

Instead of trying to tough it out, we need to show ourselves compassion, especially in a storm. It takes courage to face the overwhelm. Avoiding or fighting it often only heightens our sensitivity to it. For me, I learned new ways to go through it and cope better with my anxiety. I learned to ride the wave, and, in the process, I found my "calm."

The Power of Breathing

In Brené Brown's book *Braving the Wilderness: The Quest for True Belonging and the Courage to Stand Alone,* she shares the value of the inhale of a breath—and likens it to being still or taking the time to collect yourself and rest [1].

"...There is the in-breath and there is the out-breath. It's easy to believe we must exhale all the time, without ever inhaling. But the inhale is essential if you want to continue to exhale."

Often in life we're too focused on the exhale—the doing, the striving, and achievement. We go full speed ahead, forgetting about the inhale, the softer side of breathing. It's our reset, it's our 'calm' and just as important as the exhale. If we don't allow ourselves a full inhale, we lack oxygen, or balance. A full inhale allows us to have a full exhale.

When activated in fight-or-flight, our amygdala (again our "lizard brain"), tends to hijack the prefrontal cortex. It's a form of safety, to alert us when danger is present. While we want it to respond in appropriate situations, it can sound a false alarm and keeps us from accessing the logical side of our brain when we're not in any danger. When we're anxious, sometimes we say, "I can't think clearly." The reason we literally can't, is because our amygdala—the reptilian part of our brain—has the steering wheel.

If our brain remains in this state, it is hard for us to calm down. Understanding this helps make sense of why stressful situations or moments of overwhelm are the worst times to make decisions. However, there are simple practices we can implement to help with this.

In *Your Survival Instinct Is Killing You*, referenced in an earlier chapter, Dr. Marc Schoen shared that we all have a pain tolerance. Similarly, we also have a tolerance level or threshold to overwhelm and agitation. When our tolerance level to overwhelm is high, we don't get as rattled as someone who has a lower tolerance to overwhelm.

Dr. Schoen says we have the ability to raise our tolerance level by becoming more self-aware of how we operate within our body. He says it starts by looking at the story we're holding on to and examining our beliefs about what's happened to help us decide how we want to move forward. I want to share with you three strategies that helped me learn to breathe deep and find my 'calm', as identified in Figure 7.

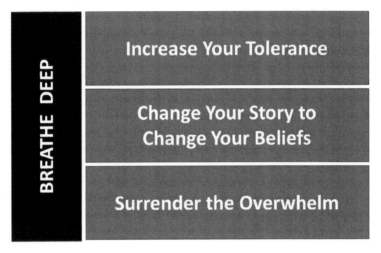

Figure 7 – Three Strategies to Breathing Deep

Increase Your Tolerance

We never know what life will throw at us, but we can build resilience to help us not only endure those moments but come out stronger. Here are four ways to increase your tolerance level.

4. Reorient Yourself

Finding one area in the body that is comfortable can help desensitize us to the overwhelm. It's called reorienting. For example, let's say you're preparing for a speech in front of a group of people; you are feeling overwhelmed and your heart is racing and your face is flushed. Take just a few seconds to personally label that uncomfortable emotion, then quickly find something that *is* comfortable on or around you—maybe your shoes, the warmth of your sweater, or the temperature in the room. Focus on that for just a few seconds and you'll find yourself making a shift. It may not be a big shift, but the idea is to take tiny steps like this to orient and remind yourself that overwhelm and comfort *can* exist simultaneously. Over time this raises your tolerance level.

2. Be Still

Many people have found that focusing on the present moment, with as little distractions as possible, is a great way to reduce overwhelm. I've found that meditation or being mindful about what's happening in that moment helps with this, whether it's paying attention while I'm eating or just sitting outside by our firepit. I notice the sounds, smells, scenery. If my mind starts jumping around, there is no judgment, I just notice it and move on. Learning to be present has helped me with my focus, reeling in my emotions and then releasing them.

Meditation, as research shows, does in fact calm the brain, and increases blood flow, improving the ability to focus even during stressful situations. Even just five minutes a day can help calm the mind.

3. Try Something New

Doing something we haven't done before, like a new hobby, helps the brain to build new neural pathways. It can help foster creativity and lessen the stress we sometimes feel when we're stuck in routines that don't benefit us. We can allow ourselves to become more flexible by getting comfortable with being *uncomfortable* by just trying something new.

4. Care for You

Self-care is underrated and to some it seems overindulgent, but if we're continually off-balance, we put our health and emotional needs at risk. We live in a society where it is honorable to run ourselves into the ground working endless hours while simultaneously caring for the needs of everyone around us. Then we're shocked when we feel burnout or, even worse, our health deteriorates. We don't make the connection that we've forgotten to take care of some of our most basic needs because we've left ourselves out of the equation.

If we do not honor ourselves, I don't believe we can truly honor others at full capacity. Yes, I know it seems self-focused, but I've learned you have to focus on your needs in order to be there efficiently for others. I know I'm a much better mom, wife, friend, daughter, and business owner when I put myself back in the equation.

What Is Self-Care?

Self-care is essentially anything you do to purposefully take care of your emotional, mental, and physical health. There are many things that fall into that category; truly, the list is endless. The problem is that many people wait until they are emotionally burnt out before they give themselves the attention they need. But why wait? Why not prevent it now, and why not give ourselves fuel we need along the way?

There is no right or wrong when it comes to self-care, except if you don't follow through with it. You may talk about how much you need some time off, or need to recharge, but thinking about it doesn't count! I know I just stated the obvious, yet we are experts at rationalizing, even when something is good for our own well-being.

A friend of mine makes it a point to schedule a day completely to herself every month. Sometimes it's overnight or an afternoon, and she puts it in her calendar way ahead of time.

I've adopted this habit myself and the impact has been remarkable. I come back home feeling almost like a different person, which is often a good thing! I mostly notice the difference when I get off track and skip a month or two. Otherwise, if I skip this routine, I fall back to that old self, feeling a little too stretched, drained and frankly hard to live with.

If staying overnight somewhere is too big a stretch for you, schedule something, even if it's just starting with five minutes a day in a locked bathroom to have some quiet time (and *yes*, I've done that too!). Put it in *ink* on your calendar so you're not tempted to change it.

What Fills You?

The best way to follow through once you've scheduled a self-care routine is to create a list of ideas for self-care to have on hand from which you can quickly choose. Here are questions you can ask yourself to spur creativity:

- What feeds your soul?

- What are the little joys in life that excite you?

- What are some activities that give you quick doses of energy?

- What are some longer activities you can do to recharge completely?

Maybe for you it's scheduling a monthly massage, taking a walk during lunchtime, going on a bike ride, watching a chick flick, kayaking, starting a new hobby, having a date night, or giving yourself permission to take off work a few hours early; again, the list is endless.

These are all simple ways we can take care of ourselves and lessen the impact of chronic stress, which often reveals itself when we press through or endure stressful situations too long. While we can't completely prevent overwhelm, we can do things to help us bounce back more quickly. According to *Harvard Business Review,* "Resilience is about how you recharge, not how you endure." [2] So instead of waiting until you're completely burnt out, practice self-care in short and regular increments to stay recharged.

Change Your Story to Change Your Beliefs

Karen is married to a police officer who was injured in the line of duty. Her husband now lives with physical and emotional challenges, which require frequent care. He now depends on Karen to take care of many of the responsibilities he once managed.

She quickly recognized that she needed to be very intentional about taking care of herself. She created her own boundaries so she wouldn't stay in a constant state of overwhelm. She often recharges herself by giving herself permission to read alone for an hour. Even though it wasn't easy at first, this simple action of self-care has helped her stay centered.

She recognizes the reality of their situation, but she gave up the notion that their life had to be a straight line with no bumps. She knew there would always be struggles, so she decided to enjoy their new life no matter what. She accepted that their journey was not going to be perfect and it would be a "crooked road." But she became determined to have fun in the process.

Karen chose to look at her situation differently, even though neither she nor her husband were at fault for what happened. She stays the course with laughter, celebrates growth along the way, and takes care of herself as she continues to support her husband and family.

Surrender the Overwhelm

Imagine for a moment you're in a high state of burnout or overwhelm. You're going full throttle, didn't check in with yourself early enough, and now you're feeling the intensity. Here are a few things you can still do.

1. Create a "Thrival Kit"

In the same way we have first-aid kits ready for when accidents happen, we can create an emotional first-aid kit to help us thrive and shift into a calmer state. Bonnie St. John, author of *Micro-Resilience: Minor Shifts for Major Boosts in Focus, Drive, and Energy,* works with organizations and teams to create their own "Survival Kit" to help during stressful times at work [3].

This is something you prepare ahead of time and you can make it out of anything. I used a large zipper pouch. Inside I put things that have special meaning to me. I have pictures of loved ones (including my dogs), my fuzzy socks, and a mastermind coin from Paraguay. I also have a favorite playlist on my phone to play whenever I need to calm myself. I bring it with me while I'm traveling. Anything that can help calm the senses (especially sound, touch, and smell) can help calm the nervous system.

2. Shift to the Big Picture

When we're stuck in the details, including anxious thoughts, we can only see the little picture. I had a friend recently remind me to recognize when I'm doing this and literally stop and think about the big picture. It's always different from what I'm experiencing at the moment. I then tell myself that even though this moment is difficult something good is also going on, and then I focus on one good thing, even if it takes me a while to name it.

When I do this, I am able to see things from a different perspective. The circumstances may not have change yet, but I start to get more creative about finding solutions to things I thought were unsolvable. This starts by shifting to the big picture.

3. *Set Boundaries*

Healthy boundaries are crucial for any relationship, especially with family members, as often those around us can impact our peace and calm if we're not prepared. For example, Denise is the caretaker for her aging mom. While she makes it a priority to take care of herself, there are times it gets overwhelming. It would be easy for her to give in, but instead of putting herself last, she asks herself often, *"What is the one thing I can do for myself today?"* Then she does it, even if it's the only thing she can do at the time. She chooses to focus on the small steps, which are enough to sustain her and build resilience.

Denise also learned she could not meet every single need of her mom; she could only do what she reasonably could. Often as a parent or caregiver, we take an all-nurturing approach—we try to do everything for our loved ones, whether it's for our kids or parents. When it seems we're not meeting their demands, we feel we're falling short or not doing an adequate job, and then we try to do more. But this causes us to fall further out of balance, putting our well-being and ourselves at risk.

Denise has learned at times to say "no" to her mom and not let her mom's overwhelm control her. Setting boundaries for our loved ones can be hard and it may hurt their feelings, but it can be the best thing for them and for us. We are not good to anyone if we don't give ourselves permission to take care of our needs.

4. Answer Your Calling

I've met managers, parents, and teachers who often feel the pull between their dreams and their family or business. They feel they have to choose one over the other. I believe that if we feel called to something outside our family or work, there is a way to do both, but we can find a way to make it doable for us and our loved ones and it will look very different than someone else's journey.

I've felt firsthand the desire to be there for my family while simultaneously pursuing other things I felt God calling me to do. There were years I put my dreams on hold during difficult seasons with my family, and there were times I made both work. You have to decide what works best for you and the season you're in.

A Lesson from an Imperfect Parent

As a mom, I desired to be the best parent I could be. I wanted to always be there for my family as well as work in a career that I love, but I feared what other moms would think. I think sometimes we fear that others think that our aspirations and dreams are selfish. I felt the pressure to stay at home with my children because that's what most of my friends did. While I didn't have a problem with other moms working outside the home, I often felt selfish for wanting to do something in addition to raising my children. Quite a tug of war, huh?

So, it was very confusing, and the guilt came up for even having a desire to work outside the home. Finally, a year and a half after giving birth to my oldest son, I went back to work part time. You could say I had the best of both worlds, but even then, I got some flak from church friends, and I had a fellow mom who I respected tell me she didn't think I was being a good mom and that I would regret my decision.

Even though at the time it was painful to face rejection from these moms, it gave me a new appreciation for working moms. We should never question a mother's heart for her family if she desires to work outside the home. Nor should we question a mom's heart if she desires to stay home. What business is it of ours in the first place to question another's heart for wanting to be their best self and happier?

We need to be more supportive of those who answer the call from their dreams and aspirations, we need to learn from their example. Instead of questioning their motives, why not ask "How can I support you?" Sometimes we do decide to put our dreams on hold, or have to out of necessity because of an unexpected circumstance. But we don't have to totally eliminate them.

So, what is your heart calling you to do now, even if you aren't able to go "all in" in your current season? What is that you want?

The Process of Surrender

Raising my children has been the most important season in my life, and even though they are now adults, I still take parenting seriously. After all, I'll always be their mom and they can't get rid of me that easily!

There have been some wonderful years and some that were more difficult. Both of my sons have mild physical challenges and when they were young, I spent a great deal of time researching medical studies and therapies so I could get the best care for them. There were times I went overboard like a crazy lady. Looking back, it was also how I coped with feelings of inadequacy as a parent.

When one of my sons went through some severe trauma, I felt helpless. We had to pull him out of school. Days turned into weeks, then into months. I found myself taking on his suffering, and I went into a depression.

I couldn't focus on anything, so I took a sabbatical from my business. My husband and I agreed I needed to start taking better care of myself, and one day I decided to get away for a week at the beach, all by myself.

You'd think I'd be jumping up and down and excited about the opportunity. But no. When I got there, I found myself immediately worrying that something would happen to my son while I was gone. I didn't know how to be with myself, have fun, or relax, as I had been in caretaker mode for months. But it was exactly what I needed to get out from under the pull of the undercurrent that was drowning me.

That week I allowed myself to release emotions that I had stuffed down for years. In those first couple of days, I went through several tissue boxes; you think I'm kidding! And I felt incredible relief. I didn't have to be strong in front of anyone, I just let myself be me. I can't describe the feeling of weight that was lifted.

I knew that once I came back home, I would be thrown again into the overwhelming role of being a caretaker. So, before I left the beach house, I decided I would find a way to make peace with my life and the situation. I realized the only thing I could really control was my attitude. I surrendered my son to God.

I wish I could tell you that I let go completely, that I felt complete relief. The truth is I had to continually release and surrender my overwhelm and worry each time they came up. There were times I still tried to control situations, but over time I relaxed more. I stopped reacting to situations with worry, I recognized when

I was enabling. I now allow both my children to walk their own journey. I'm here to help, but not to live it for them. The joy and peace we can experience when we let go of trying to control the outcomes is freeing.

We can sometimes help, but we can't fix people, nor should we try. While people's behavior can often use improving, I personally don't believe *they themselves* need to be fixed. An incessant need to fix people's situations silently communicates that we don't believe in them. Our role should instead be to guide, love, and accept them, and not to over-interfere or rob them of the opportunity to self-discover and grow. This is one of the hardest things to learn as a parent—at least for me as it's hard to see our loved ones suffer. But as I found we often create more suffering or create our own suffering by trying to make life overly easy for others.

Takeaways

Breathe Deep is an important component to giving yourself permission. In this chapter, I shared the following strategies:

- **Don't fight overwhelm. Embrace it.** When you're in full panic mode, stop and get back into the moment. Shift to big-picture thinking and remember this will pass. Ride the wave.

- **Learn to breathe more efficiently.** When you feel overwhelmed, change your breathing pattern. Slowing down your breath can power down your heart rate, which leads to calmness. Try yoga and meditation to help you stay in the habit of controlling your breath.

- **Increase your tolerance level.** While you can't get rid of all the stress of overwhelming situations, there are things you can do to bounce back more quickly when overwhelm does show up.

- **Manage overwhelm with new systems.** Create safeguards, like a "Thrival Kit," to help you manage your overwhelm. These external devices can help you change your state in an instant when you need it.

- **It doesn't have to be either/or.** You can still give yourself permission to care for your family, and pursue your dreams. They are not mutually exclusive. Stop thinking either/or and start thinking both/and.

- **Create healthy boundaries.** People closest to you can be your biggest source of support or your largest liability. Teach them how the relationship will be conducted, and if that's not respected, politely decline to go overboard in meeting needs that lead to enabling and codependency.

- **Trust the plan.** You can surrender, let go, and make peace with your season even when things seem hopeless. Trust that your seasons will come and go, and that even during the difficult ones, joy and growth are possible.

Dig Deeper

- What are some things that overwhelm you?

- What are some helpful tools you could use to support you with this?

- What are some boundaries needed when it comes to others?

- Have there been times when you've felt the pull between loved ones and responsibilities, which put your dreams on hold?

- If so, what are some small steps you can take to keep your dreams alive even during your current season?

Chapter 8
Have Fun

Let go of taking life too seriously

Never, ever underestimate the importance of having fun.

— Randy Pausch

We attended a Bible study group years ago and enjoyed connecting with some of the other couples. There was one mom I wanted to get to know more and one day I asked what she did for fun. She flashed a look of annoyance and growled, "Fun? I don't have time for fun. I have five kids."

I appreciated her honesty, and I think many can relate to her, even if they're not a mother, especially those who are responsible for projects and people on a day-to-day operation. You're the "main engine," and if anything gets off track, you're stuck with getting the train back on the rails.

We truly want to enjoy life, but the truth is we often sacrifice our joy to satisfy the needs of others. We do what it takes to get the job done even if we become misaligned in the process.

But, do you remember when you were young and barely had any responsibilities? Then you graduated from school, went to college, got that full-time job, started a family, and everything changed. Suddenly your time became limited and regular fun became optional. It doesn't have to be this way. Life is meant to be enjoyed on a regular basis. Not that we should ignore our responsibilities or people, but when did it become okay to only enjoy life on special occasions?

There can be things that temporarily steal our joy, but if we focus on intentionally rebuilding our joy, we can restore it and have reserves for those times we feel depleted. These strategies are identified in Figure 8.

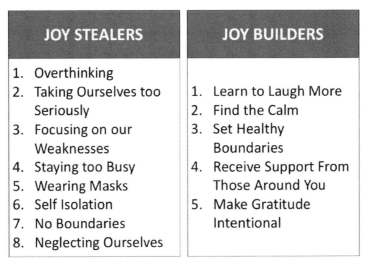

JOY STEALERS	JOY BUILDERS
1. Overthinking 2. Taking Ourselves too Seriously 3. Focusing on our Weaknesses 4. Staying too Busy 5. Wearing Masks 6. Self Isolation 7. No Boundaries 8. Neglecting Ourselves	1. Learn to Laugh More 2. Find the Calm 3. Set Healthy Boundaries 4. Receive Support From Those Around You 5. Make Gratitude Intentional

Figure 8 – Strategies for Having Joy

What's Stealing Your Joy?

If you manage a team or company, have a family, or take care of other people, you might understand the point I'm making. Those under our responsibility lean on us and we often sacrifice our wants and needs for theirs. While there are times we need to make sacrifices, it should never be at the expense of our joy. When we're in a state of joy, we're more accessible to others, more confident, more productive, and resourceful.

In my early years of motherhood, I would proudly devote most of my time and energy to serving my family, but sometimes in the same breath I would begrudgingly think I never had enough time to myself, and that I rarely got a chance to breathe. I felt resentment, and then would feel guilty thinking I didn't have a right to feel that way because my husband worked hard so we could live comfortably. I kept it to myself, letting the resentment build, not realizing or admitting I had choices.

It can sometimes be overwhelming when others are dependent on you. It requires you to put their needs at the forefront and we can easily get off-balance and forget to meet our own needs; then we get caught up in a pattern of overextending ourselves and coming face-to-face with burnout. Think of someone you know who has sacrificed to the point where their physical and emotional health was compromised.

In taking the journey of living boldly and fully, it isn't easy to admit that we can get caught in a cycle of demands, responsibilities, and sometimes self-martyrdom, and forget about creating the life that's been offered to us.

One way to keeping ourselves fueled while creating our dream and helping others in our path is simply by "enjoying the journey" more. This phrase has become a watered-down cliché, but its essence holds true. It can keep us from running on empty even in the most difficult times. Even small, frequent doses of joy can sustain us in the darkest of times. We no longer have to wait 'til we are too burnt out to pay attention to joy and fun. We can act now. As in this very minute.

When we don't enjoy our journey, we lose sight of our purpose. Things that we were once passionate about can become a chore and resentment can build. We become so preoccupied with what life gives us, we forget what gives us life. There are also some underlying culprits that prevent us from enjoying the journey:

1. Overthinking

When we think too much on something, we become over-focused on a problem, and in doing so we literally overtax our brains. We get inside our heads too much and focus only on what seems logical, and we forget about utilizing the creative side of our brains. We limit our brains to left-brain functionality. This makes us resistant to new ideas, thoughts, and angles, at which the right side of our brains is very efficient.

2. Taking Ourselves and Life Too Seriously

I can easily take myself and life too seriously. I love solving things and I can easily get stuck in my thoughts and forget to have fun. It's not because I don't like to have fun, because I do, I just have to remind myself to relax. When you get off-balance in any area, you have to intentionally remember to include the other areas. In this case, it's remembering to let yourself be light-hearted.

3. Focusing on Our Weaknesses

When we're over-focused on our weaknesses, it makes our flaws feel giant-sized. We'll exaggerate the tiniest weaknesses, making them much bigger than they really are. When we take the focus off our weaknesses and focus on our strengths, it changes our view and we're able to see things more clearly. By allowing ourselves to have more fun, we see the big picture—the goodness of life and the miracles we miss by being focused only on our hardships.

4. Staying Too Busy

Our culture rewards and idolizes busyness. We're always doing something and always have some place to go. There's a part of us that already knows we need to slow down, but we fear we might be viewed as lazy and unproductive. We pride ourselves in getting things done, but if left unchecked we can lose ourselves and become unglued. Our over-availability, "I'll be here for you 24/7," way of thinking is highly valued, but not without us paying a price—in the form of exhaustion and fear of letting people down. Our desire for approval and for people to see us as 100% dependable becomes a higher priority than our balance and well-being.

5. Wearing Masks

Masks keep us from remembering who we are and fully enjoying those who we're with. Our fear of exposing our flaws and ourselves creates walls between us and those with whom we desire to connect. Once we give ourselves permission to be ourselves and not feel ashamed of our quirks, there is huge freedom; we realize we don't have to work so hard and we can let our guard down.

6. Creating Self-Isolation

We can be surrounded by people and yet still feel alone. I felt this way in my younger motherhood years, but you never would've known it because I was good at putting a smile on my face. The truth is I often felt left out and disconnected from other women. I was too busy having my own pity party instead of trying to be a friend. It wasn't until I started accepting myself and seeing my own worth that I started making the effort to connect with other people more.

7. Having No Boundaries

Other people's demands hold us captive when we don't have clear, healthy boundaries and it makes it harder to enjoy the journey. Here's the kicker, though: We've allowed it. We aren't victims, we're giving others permission to encroach on our freedom and choices. Setting boundaries and learning to say "no" returns your power to you.

8. *Neglecting to Take Care of Ourselves*

We daily need to remind ourselves that we deserve love and care just like everyone else. For example, my husband failing to take time to enjoy the journey caused him to neglect his health. He wasn't getting the sleep he needed, wasn't eating the right foods on a daily basis. The combination of 5-hour nights of sleep, caffeinated soda, and fast food sandwiches took a toll. If we don't take care of ourselves (and no one is going to remind us), then others will end up taking care of *us*.

What's Building Your Joy?

Now that we know the things that can rob us of our joy, let's now explore some key ways to restore it.

1. *Learn to Laugh More*

Learn to laugh at yourself and life as you are going through it. Let's face it: Life unscripted is going to have some twists and turns. It can be hard to laugh at ourselves in the middle of a crisis. But we still need to be intentional and create those interruptions. Often, we create more of a crisis when we refuse to see the good side of things. So why must we wait until a crisis is over to laugh?

Tony Robbins shares that if something is going to be funny a few years from now, why not laugh about it today? When we're able to laugh at even our most embarrassing moments, it eases uncomfortable atmospheres [1].

When we take life too seriously, we make life harder than it needs to be—and it's already hard enough! When you feel yourself getting too serious, or taking something too personally, take a comedy break, a literal one. *I Love Lucy* is my go-to. I'll watch it and laugh until I feel better. Studies prove that laughter changes our body's chemistry. So next time you are caught in an awkward moment, try laughing at yourself or the situation and see how it changes things.

2. Find the Calm

If you spend any time with me, you know I love kayaking. As much as I talk about it, you'd think I was very skilled or an expert in braving the rapids, but I tend to avoid rough water. I prefer to paddle in flat water where it's calm.

Life is often about braving the rapids, but life can be found in the calm too. Learn to let go and enjoy peaceful moments and give yourself permission to not continually be on the go. There are many opportunities to enjoy the peace and calm; the choice is yours whether you take it or not.

3. Set Healthy Boundaries

Healthy boundaries clearly define relationships so that life works better for both parties. Boundaries may feel limiting at first, and you may have some pushback from those you set a boundary with, but they can be empowering.

Let's say we decide to set a boundary and let our boss know that we're not available after work hours or on weekends. This is where we easily talk ourselves out of what we agreed to as soon as we get an email on a Saturday. We have a choice to keep our boundary or not. Just know that each time you don't comply with your own boundary, the receiving end won't take it seriously either. Communicating clearly is essential and then following through is just as important.

In *Boundaries for Leaders: Results, Relationships, and Being Ridiculously in Charge,* author Dr. Henry Cloud shares how high-performance teams have clear boundaries in place for their team members and themselves [2]. And without these boundaries they would not be able to function optimally or be as productive.

4. Receive Support from Those Around You

There were many years I didn't ask for help, whether I was struggling in school, learning a new job, or needing help with my children. I felt admitting I needed help was a sign of weakness. I couldn't have been more wrong, and gratefully so. I've seen others struggle with this. Too often we wouldn't think twice about helping someone else but when it comes to our own needs, we instantly think that we're burdening someone.

In the last 10 years, I've reached out for help more than the last three decades. While occasionally someone will say "no", most of the time people have been overjoyed and excited to help. I had to give myself permission, though, to let go of my pride and belief that I had to do things on my own.

There are times we need to be independent, and times we can to ask for help, and there's no shame in it. By opening ourselves up to receive support from others, we create deeper connections and more moments of joy.

5. Make Gratitude Intentional

We've heard that being grateful can make you feel better in a difficult situation, but did you know there is evidence that it is physically good for you? A study by Alex Wood, Jeffrey Froh, and Adam Geraghty helps support this idea [3].

Their study showed that practicing "thankfulness" reduced risks of certain disorders such as major depression, generalized anxiety disorder, and drug abuse. It has also helped people adjust to life after traumatic events and improved overall feelings of well-being [4].

I created a "gratitude" album that I keep on my office shelf. It is filled with things that I'm grateful for—handwritten cards from my mom and friends, thank you cards from clients, and pictures of things that make me happy. When I'm feeling down, I grab the book and I look through it, read, and in a few minutes my spirits are lifted, and I can see the big picture much clearer.

A Lesson on Burning the Candle at Both Ends

Our expectations of work also play a big role in stealing our joy. If you're not careful, the "job" can easily rob the "joy" of not just you, but those around you too.

My husband gave me permission to share his perspective of his struggle with this. Many men take great pride in their work. It creates for them a sense of identity, and because of that, they want to do their best with their work and make an impact. That desire, though, can be hard to just turn off. A typical 8-hour day can easily become a 12- to 16-hour day. My husband's drive to accomplish, to succeed at work, has been hard to turn off—especially in the early years of our marriage. Little did he know the impact his overworking was having not only on himself, but on our family. For a period of time, our relationship suffered. It was less than optimal. And his health also suffered.

In hindsight, he wishes he could go back and readjust. He wishes he could go tell the younger version of himself the importance of giving yourself permission to take off work, to take more family trips together and to let work just wait another day. He now shares with others today that, "The job, as important as it is, isn't as nearly as important as the joy of the journey with your family."

Takeaways

- **Enjoy the journey.** Ultimately you are in control of your life, your relationships, and your reactions to both. Infuse joy in everything. The journey will be as fun as you allow it to be.

- **Watch for energy pitfalls.** These are things that can take the fun out of life and leave you that sour feeling. Some pitfalls are self-inflicted and others is what we allow to happen to us. The thing to do is to always check your emotions.

- **Laugh at yourself.** Don't take yourself too seriously. Have a chuckle at your own expense and you'll find that life lightens up.

- **Set boundaries.** It's not about walling yourself in and keeping others out. Boundaries exist so that relationships can thrive with basic rules that help each person respect one another more. There is freedom and joy when you draw clear lines.

- **Ask for support.** Ask questions and be open to input. We grow deeper connections when we're helping each other. Don't fear asking questions to get answers you don't know. It will save you frustration from making unnecessary errors.

- **Chase joy.** Life won't be a 50/50 balance, but you can find harmony and joy in any situation. Take the cards you were dealt, create a new game, and have fun while you're at the table!

Dig Deeper

- Do you sometimes take life too seriously? If so, what are some ways you could have more fun?

- Who and what brings you joy?

- Who could you reach out to for support and encouragement?

- What is one small way you can bring gratitude into your life daily?

Chapter 9
Pay Forward

Leading others creates an ongoing ripple effect

> *Your story is the greatest legacy that you will*
> *leave to your friends. It's the longest-lasting*
> *legacy you will leave to your heirs.*

— Steve Saint

The first step into bold living happens when you realize you don't want to stay where you currently are. It doesn't mean that you aren't thankful for what you have, but you sense there is more to be discovered and more to give. When you make the decision to be BOLD, it goes beyond just the impact it has on you.

The growth we experience in living a bold life is the catalyst to a fuller life and a better you. If we choose to keep the growth to ourselves, we lose the contentment and others miss out. That's because our dreams and goals aren't just meant for us, they are meant to be shared. In sharing our dreams, we create opportunities for others and inspire them to live their lives boldly.

The Big Picture Revisited

Imagine for a moment not being able to communicate through language; that somehow your ability to verbally speak has been turned off or limited. What's frustrating is that your intelligence—how you process, crunch numbers, recall memories, and dream—is still there. You just can't express it. That would affect your life significantly, wouldn't it?

The condition I'm describing, aphasia, is very real for over two million Americans who are affected by it due to an injury to the brain, usually through stroke, head trauma, or brain tumor. Most people aren't familiar with it, yet it is more common than Parkinson's disease, cerebral palsy, and muscular dystrophy [1].

Those who have aphasia have extreme difficulty communicating, understanding speech, and reading and writing. And yet their intelligence remains intact. Imagine the frustration they must feel not being able to articulate their thoughts or properly connect with those around them. But imagine if there was a way that they could be helped.

One of my most rewarding pursuits is collaborating with a team that has dedicated their work to solving problems such as isolation. They are using technology in conjunction with traditional therapies to help people like those who are affected by aphasia [2].

Their desire is to help those with the condition to better connect with their families and communities so that they can reengage with the world. It's given them a new hope.

Using our gifts to help others in and of itself becomes a gift. It gives us added purpose and helps us stay focused on the bigger picture. When you live your life with meaning every day, it fuels you, especially during difficult seasons.

Some of the actions on living in the bigger picture and benefits of paying it forward are identified in Figure 9.

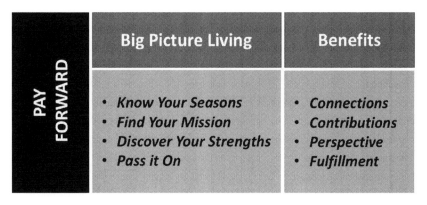

Figure 9 – Actions and Benefits to Paying it Forward

1. *Know Your Seasons*

When my children were struggling with various challenges, I understood part of my journey was to help them through theirs. It became the most important season at the time. I've also known that there was more for me to do one day.

While motherhood has been very fulfilling for me, I could almost hear God periodically whispering to me, *"But wait, there's more! For now, be present in the season you're in."* When I started viewing my life as a set of seasons, it changed the way I looked at things.

Sometimes we like the season we're in and other times the season is difficult and painful. In the book *The Seasons of Life* by Jim Rohn, he compares the four seasons to our personal seasons [3]. We can learn something from them, even the hardest ones. While winter can be brutal, it's also a time for rest and preparation for the spring when there is new growth. There are things we can do in every season to make the most of it and prepare for the next one.

2. *Find Your Mission*

In order to navigate through our seasons, it's helpful to define what the mission of each season is. While it seems like we'll be in some seasons forever, they eventually transition into a new one then we have new missions. For example, raising my children to be healthy and independent was my mission for many years. While my mission is still my family, I'm in a new season of growth with my business, and my clients are now part of my mission. What is your mission for the current season you're in?

3. *Discover Your Strengths*

When you surround yourself with people who are intentionally growing in their lives, they will challenge you to grow. They will see things inside you that you don't yet see. Have these people help you identify your strengths.

Other than being told that I was a good listener, I didn't know what other strengths I had. When I surrounded myself with people who ahead of me, I asked them what they felt my strengths were. I listened to them and realized I had discounted some of my gifts. I started to embrace my strengths the more I used them.

Everyone has been given strengths, but not everyone knows what they are. It's up to each of us to find them and use them and pass them on to others. The key is once you discover a strength, use it and develop it to full capacity. When you do, you'll find other strengths you didn't know you had.

4. *Pass It On*

As I got comfortable coming out of my shell, I began sharing my growth with others through coaching and retreats. As I became more open about my own struggles, it encouraged people to know that they didn't have to have it all together.

Like a pebble cast into a pond, you can create a ripple effect that influences others. Living boldly and breaking free of labels creates opportunities for you to help others live boldly. Instead of asking "Why me?" ask "Why not me?" By giving yourself permission to choose your growth and share it with others, you can start a never-ending ripple.

Benefits of Paying it Forward

We have the power to create exponential growth, but it's only possible if we choose to pay it forward to others. We can share our story of not only our successes in life, but our failures, fears, and how we learned to grow from them.

Our victories may be impressive, yet it's often being open about our struggles that helps us connect with someone's heart. Here are some ways we can give the person behind us a leg up as we continue to advance forward.

1. Greater Connections

Growth starts with you, but it doesn't have to stop with you. You can influence others in their growth by connecting with them and building relationships. Connection requires you to reach out to others. We can encourage them in their journey. Encouragement, as it is defined, allows us to pour courage into others. Courage is a quality of someone choosing to be bold. When we encourage, we are triggering activators of growth, because growth comes only when we choose to be bold. By connecting with others in this way, we can help them find greater meaning in their lives. We can help them in their seasons and on their missions, and ultimately help them pursue the bigger picture.

2. *Greater Contributions*

Most people want to add value and give back, and this can be done in countless ways. While money is commonly contributed and can provide opportunities for others, lending your gifts and strengths through service can empower them, sometimes even further than financial assistance. In addition to your gifts and strengths, your vision can also spark something inside people, giving them hope in their pursuit of life. As a person of growth, what can you do to give someone an opportunity to enrich their lives too?

3. *Greater Perspective*

When you pay it forward, you begin to see the world differently. It becomes less about you and more about the bigger picture, and you realize you are more connected to others than you previously thought. While we may have completely different experiences from each other, we have all experienced pain, love, and joy. When we make a difference in someone else's world, it models for them how to make a difference for someone else. Suddenly we see how our influence on one person becomes a ripple. Our influence is much greater than we realize.

By choosing to not share our growth with someone, we not only rob that person of an opportunity, we may be robbing many people of potential growth and opportunities. When I realized the impact of my inaction, it struck me like an arrow through my heart. Giving yourself permission to live fully goes way beyond yourself and is part of a much bigger mission.

4. *Greater Fulfillment*

We want to have a sense of purpose and fulfillment, and when we don't, we tend to fill that void with temporary things that seem to make us happy. These can be things like material belongings, our lifestyle, and unhealthy habits and addictions, including staying busy or obsessively going after goals. But when we start seeking meaning, we find we are less concerned about the petty things, and have more energy to focus on leading others.

Passing the Torch of Boldness

Before we are able to pass on what we have learned in our growth, we first have to define what boldness means to us and show that we have been living it. The perfect place to be bold is to leverage our experiences to help others through their journeys. It can increase our capacity to help and add value to others. Each step of growth gives us more to offer others and more experiences to share.

We often hear about leaving a lasting legacy. When we are intentional about leaving a legacy, we are strategizing how we can live beyond our physical years so that others carry out the lessons we've instilled in them after we're gone. So, think about what mark you want to leave on this world. A mark that will continue on living way after you've gone. What does that look like?

Some people think having pictures and family albums are enough, so people can look through them and remember us. Others want an inspirational epitaph on their tombstones. Those are both nice and meaningful, but if you crave a lasting legacy that transforms lives, it requires planning.

Yes, this is where things get a little uncomfortable—because we're talking about after you've passed through those pearly gates. But if you want to continue your message, start now by living more boldly and finding a way to have others involved with your dream— because your dream becomes your legacy. There's a saying that drives this point: "What you leave behind is not what is engraved in stone monuments, but what is woven into the lives of others."

So, how do you leave your mark? What does that uniquely look like for you? Only you can answer that. There are many ways to pass on our story and growth. Think about someone who has passed on that has left a legacy you admire. What have they done?

For me, I've chosen to mentor and coach people who have a strong desire to continue making this world a better place. They will continue to grow and pass on their growth; some call this the butterfly effect. I don't have to be here forever in order for the change that I start to continue. Remember the ripple.

Another way I've chosen to pass on my legacy is through this book. I hope it will encourage future generations. My hope is that something within these pages will spark you to give yourself permission to live your life fully and create a bold legacy that continues to your ripple.

I remember how much my mom believed in me during my early years. Often, the seeds a mom plants take root at a young age, but some don't sprout and bear fruit until much later. I share that again to remind you to never underestimate a seed that's planted in someone else's life. It may not seem like it has taken root, but there is always the hope that it will.

We are the sower of seeds. We are not responsible for their growth, that's between them and God, but we can be the vessel. If that person is open, that seed's going to find a way.

Bringing Out Your Best

Remember when I shared earlier about the Parable of the Talents and one servant dug a hole and buried his? That parable haunted me for many years. I knew I had God-given gifts, but I didn't know what they were. It frustrated me, as it seemed like other people knew theirs and understood how to make a difference using them. They were shining. They had great success. And then there was me.

I was like the man who buried his talents only I didn't know *where* I buried them! I had to go on a personal scavenger hunt to find them. While the process wasn't always fun, there were many people who came into my path to help me. Through their encouragement, I learned from my experiences and started believing in myself.

Discovering and investing my talents both in others and myself drives me to this day. I have a responsibility to my children, to my clients, and to the world to be my best. And on the days when I'm not at my best, I've learned that this is okay too, because there is always tomorrow. It leads me to into the happiness mentioned in the Parable—the place where God smiles on you for using what He has given you to build others up.

Takeaways

- **Recognize the seasons.** There are seasons in life. You can meet the needs of those important to you without giving away your dreams. You were put here to leave a legacy outside of your comfort zone.

- **Boldness means clarifying your mission.** We feel alive when we live in our purpose. Remember life has multiple seasons with different missions. Play the long game by looking beyond the season you are in.

- **Start your ripple.** Once you begin to boldly live a life of meaning, share your life with others. You have the power to create change that goes beyond just your life.

- **Shine brightly.** God gave you tremendous strengths. Put them to use. Find and develop them. Don't hide or bury them. Then help others find their strengths too.

Dig Deeper

- In what ways could you multiply your growth by spreading it to others?
- What gifts skills can you develop more?
- What legacy do you want to leave in the world?
- What can you do to prepare for your legacy?

Chapter 10
Lead On

Make leading yourself a lifetime goal

---

*Do something today that your future self will
thank you for.*

— Unknown

After high school, I went away to college at Liberty University in Lynchburg, Virginia. I loved that first year of college life; feeling a new sense of freedom for the first time was exciting. It was also the first time I felt comfortable making friends. Part of that was no one knew my past, and it was like starting life with a clean slate. My roommates and I got along well; there were lots of laughter and pranks. Although my classes were challenging, I managed to keep up with my busy schedule.

About the same time, I started dating Paul (now my husband), who lived back in my hometown. During the summer after my freshman year, I went with him to visit his family in South Carolina. They had recently bought a beautiful but somewhat "green" horse that wasn't ridden a lot. Knowing I had some experience with riding, they offered for me to take him out in a large field.

While I was riding, something spooked him. The horse took off, running with me hanging on as tight as I could. After thinking I finally had him under control, he bucked me off and I went cartwheeling into the air. My body slammed on the ground, leaving me with a lower broken back.

When I returned to Liberty in the fall, I felt "off." Not only because my back was still healing, but my mind felt scrambled. I struggled that semester to stay on top of my grades, I couldn't focus, and I was extremely homesick. Since my grades had slipped so much toward the end of the semester, I decided to not finish out my sophomore year and instead moved back home.

I transferred to Old Dominion University, where Paul went to school, thinking things would be different. To my surprise, I still couldn't concentrate. Eventually, my grades got so bad I withdrew from classes there too. I was frustrated and resigned myself to the idea that I just wasn't smart enough, that I wasn't college material.

About that time, my future father-in-law asked if I could work for his company near Washington, D.C., as an administrative assistant, to fill in for his assistant who was on maternity leave. It was the perfect job for me. I was trained well, had an organized routine, and worked with an extremely friendly group of people.

I learned new skills and was allowed to work at my own pace. It eventually led to a permanent job as a financial analyst. My confidence in myself grew, and I got great annual performance reviews. Life was good. Eventually Paul and I married, and, after I gave birth to our first son, I decided to go back to school to finish my degree. But I knew I couldn't go about it the same way. I was now a full-time working mother, so I decided to take things slow.

I took one class at a time—the perfect pace for me. Eight years after my first attempt at college, I finally earned a BS in Management. And to my surprise, I earned a Student of the Year Award. Through this long experience of trial and error, I learned how to develop study habits. I learned the importance of creating simple systems for memorizing content.

It reminds me that there are things in life that are tough, and while we may be tempted to quit, we can figure how to navigate around it *if* we want it bad enough.

Sometimes we focus too much on where we fall short and think we can't go beyond an obstacle. But think about people in history who discovered medical breakthroughs and found solutions that had a far-reaching impact. Many of those people faced challenges of their own. What if these people had accepted their current state or condition, not believing that they could create change? They somehow found a way to shift from what was current to what was possible.

Louis Pasteur was not an academic and failed many exams, yet he became a famous French biologist, microbiologist, and chemist and known for his discoveries of fermentation and pasteurization in vaccinations. Quite remarkable, huh? Somehow his driving force came after he lost his son to typhoid fever. What if Louis Pasteur settled for his circumstances and didn't pursue what he was passionate about? What if he settled for what seemed practical and didn't allow himself to think further than his current conditions?

We can't always reach our goals every single time, but we can restart or try something new and determine to see it through. Louis Pasteur didn't allow defeat or death stop him from finding cures for several diseases. When we allow our experiences to refine us and not define us, we can face our failures with new resolve and act in boldness. But you don't have to wait for a challenge or major life crisis to start living more boldly; you can create your own turning points *now*.

Two additional elements that will allow you to go further than you could ever imagine are identified in Figure 10 and discussed in this chapter.

	Bet on Yourself	Walk in Boldness
LEAD ON	• *Be willing to stand alone* • *Be willing to get uncomfortable* • *Be willing to start without having fully clarity* • *Be willing to mess up in front of others*	• *Develop New Habits* • *Be Accountable* • *Be Intentional* • *Develop Resilience*

Figure 10 – Core Components to Go Further

Bet on Yourself

You may not be where you want to be, but you can give yourself permission to change that today, even if it's one small step. You might be thinking of a missed opportunity you've had in your past. Give yourself permission to let it go.

Maybe you need to forgive yourself or someone else. Allow yourself to pursue another quest or opportunity without the ghost of the last one haunting you. It's your life. Take control. Keep asking yourself, "What's waiting for me?"

To help you, here are a few lessons from my college experience that has taught me what it means to lead on.

1. Be willing to stand alone

My college merry-go-round taught me about resiliency. Those times proved difficult, and in my discouragement, I wasn't a fun person to be around. When I returned to Liberty after my horseback riding accident, a others noticed there was something different about me. I was depressed, unfocused and not as much fun. I felt misunderstood. Heck, I didn't even understand myself.

I learned in time that trying to make sense of everything can be unproductive. Sometimes we don't have the answers, and sometimes we need to take time to heal. Not everyone will understand, and that's okay. Be willing to take a different path, even if it means standing alone at times.

Eventually people will come onto our new path to encourage us, but there are stretches where we need to be content to stand alone, still trusting we are on the right track. Be committed to your journey, even if it's a slow process.

2. Be willing to get uncomfortable

In time, like the hermit crab, you'll get comfortable in your new shell. Don't get too comfortable, though. Eventually it will be time to get a bigger shell, and you'll naturally continue the desire to grow. Don't fight the process. If you too find yourself feeling uncomfortable during times of growth, keep remembering your reason for doing it and keep marching forward.

3. Be willing to start without having full clarity

In Chapter 3, I shared that I've admired (and was sometimes even jealous of) people who seem to have full clarity about what they want in life. They are clear on their vision. They've got it mapped out, they know how they will get it, and it seems they easily achieve it. Me? I would get bits and pieces of my vision and often they don't fit together right away. For a long time, this would hold me back from taking the first step. I listened too much what other people were telling me—that I needed to have crystal-clear clarity before I could have confidence.

I interpreted my lack of clarity as if I was doomed for failure! Then I found out the majority of people don't have complete clarity. In fact, even for the ones who think they do, there are still things about life they haven't discovered. I decided to slow things way down. I have found that just having a little clarity is enough to get started. You can always build more along the way.

How about you? Do you sometimes struggle with feeling there is a lack of clarity in your life? Stay encouraged and keep acting in faith, focus on the one thing you are clear about and take action in that one thing.

4. *Be willing to mess up in front of others*

It used to bother me when I would mess up during a presentation. I would try to smooth it over as if nothing happened, you know, "fake it till you make it." This may work for some, For me? I'm way too easy to read.

Now, I just acknowledge my mistake, laugh at myself and move on. People want to see the real you, flaws and all. They don't want perfection; the world doesn't need the version of you where you're trying to say everything right without any "ums" and "ahs." Yes, it's important we do our best, but let people see your flaws and struggles too. That takes real guts and boldness. When you take this step, without the masks or perfection, you'll find a fearless side of yourself that you never knew existed.

There was a time I struggled with worrying that people wouldn't think I was smart enough and that I had anything to offer them. I know that sounds silly, but it's amazing how our B.S. Story fights to survive. My breakthrough came when I realized that it's not about what I know or what I say to them. It's more important about what is coming into their awareness and discovering who they are.

People need to see you being okay with your imperfections, because they need to know they're going to be okay, too. You can give them that hope. Having weaknesses is not a sign of being weak. Your willingness to not hide them can encourage them. At times our weaknesses can become a tool to lead others into their strength. Remember to bet on yourself!

Walk in Boldness

My friend Dawn was greatly struggling with her health. Her blood pressure and cholesterol were elevated. She was a borderline diabetic, and she was in constant pain from her joints aching. Then one day her wake-up call came when she received a diagnosis of endometrial cancer, which required a full hysterectomy. She realized she could either continue down the path she was taking, or she could embark on a completely new journey. Thankfully she chose the latter and made the decision to improve the quality of her health and create more balance in her life.

Previously her weight had stopped her from doing many things in her life, so she started looking more closely at what she ate and made the necessary changes. She also began to conquer her fears, develop healthy communication skills, set boundaries, and shared her journey with others, even the difficult moments. She lost 120 pounds and is now cancer-free. While she recognizes her health journey is still in process, she has committed to living boldly and encourages others to overcome their health challenges.

While we can't change everything, we can change some things. We can choose to let our struggles shape us and prepare us for what's next. We can change our habits, we can be accountable, we can be intentional, and we can develop resilience.

Here are a few tips in these four areas that can give you a solid foundation to stand on as you start moving forward in boldness.

1. *Develop New Habits*

The first step to living a bold life is developing new habits, in both how we think and how we take action. Often when we're excited about a new endeavor, we want to go "gung-ho," but it's more effective to start small with one thing we can do well consistently.

As you build that new "muscle," old habits fade and new habits form. These lead to the foundation of creating lasting change. In taking small, measurable steps, our confidence grows. We can look back and see those mile markers we achieved and celebrate how far we've come.

2. *Be Accountable*

Probably one of the most important steps is accountability. Without being accountable to someone, it's easy to drift off. When we have someone alongside us with a more objective view, they can encourage us to keep moving.

I have several accountability partners in different areas and also a coach. They challenge me, cheer me on, and help me refocus. I recommend you find someone you trust; this can be a mentor, teacher, or coach. Whoever your accountability partner is, they should understand your goals, call you out on your excuses and recognize when you're falling back into your comfort zone.

3. *Be Intentional*

It's essential that we act with intention, doing things with a purpose and not just expecting things to happen out of the blue [1]. Your intent marks *your* dream, and the purpose – as you see it -- of *your* life. Remember you are the leading role, director, editor, and producer. Give yourself permission to take control of it.

Think of intentionality as possessing a learner's permit that will let you be the driver of your life. Embrace the learner's spirit and be a student of your life. This is what it takes to be intentional.

4. Develop Resilience

Finally, as I discussed in other chapters, you will want to develop resilience. This is where you can learn to deal with those speed bumps in life. Being resilient is learning to use past pain and difficult experiences and repurpose them as fuel.

While bad days and unproductive moments come and go, you can learn to be okay with them. Every day won't be a good day, so learn to recharge often—this builds resilience and helps you to bounce back more quickly.

Okay. It's time. No more hiding. No more brushing off your desires and dreams for something more. You have within the pages of this book what you need to help you start the journey. You have everything *inside* you to become the person you were meant to be. This is the part of the race where I pass the baton to you. Are you ready to give yourself permission to be BOLD?

Takeaways

- **Don't give up.** Life can throw us curveballs. Before you believe that the problem is only with you, see if other factors outside of your control is playing a role—such as a health challenge, an unresolved issue, or other difficulties. Instead of throwing in the towel, examine everything.

- **There is no deadline on your dream.** It took three tries for me to earn my degree. It may take you some effort, energy, and several missteps to reach your goal, but remember that the focus is on learning to fall in love with the process *more* than achieving the goal. This makes reaching the goal that much sweeter.

- **Give yourself permission to be bold.** Don't wait for others to validate you and your ideas. Be intentional and take control. You were given a purpose to pursue and a dream to capture. Go forward in boldness, get the reward and keep pressing on—in boldness.

Dig Deeper

- What is your biggest takeaway from the book?

- What ONE thing are you committed to doing to live your life more boldly?

- Break that one thing down into smaller steps, create a timeline, then schedule it on your calendar.

- Identify one person who can hold you accountable for those steps; reach out to them this week and share your intentions.

The BOLD Manifesto

It's time to unleash your Inner BOLD.
It's time to live life with courage.
Start by giving yourself permission.
Permission to step BOLDLY.
Permission to be you.

Stop seeking approval from others.
Stop playing "Mother May I?"
Start playing the lead role in your story.
The life you are to live, the one that God has set for you,
is about a choice -- the choice to be BOLD!

Boldness is not a feeling,
Or a gift others will grant.
Give yourself consent.
Consent to push through obstacles.
Consent to think different and create new results.

Stand UP, let your light shine BRIGHTLY,
So that others can find their way.
You were made for a purpose.
You were made to stand TALL.
Don't apologize for being you!

Grow and grow SLOW.
Breathe and breathe DEEP.
Take time to have FUN.
You can't rush a masterpiece.

Let go of taking life too seriously.
Being present is your superpower.

Pay it FORWARD.
Create an ongoing ripple effect.
Make leading a lifetime goal.
Bet on YOU, bet on your life, bet on your future!
You have a HOPE and a DREAM.
Trust your journey, and the One who created you.

You are on a mission to love, live and lead FULLY.
Go! BE BOLD.
Leave your mark on the world!

•••

A copy of **The BOLD Manifesto** and other resources
can be accessed at www.discovernextstep.com.

Afterword

Since I started writing this book, life has been quite interesting. If you've ever prayed for patience, you know what I'm talking about. You will be faced with situations that will test your patience. For me, I prayed for resilience and clarity while writing. During much of the writing process, I started struggling with processing, extreme fatigue, and balance.

I received a couple of diagnoses, the most challenging from an old head injury that impacted my nervous system. I began to doubt my abilities, especially when it came to sharing my story and about living boldly. Plain and simple, I struggled with giving myself permission to write this book.

Then came all the thoughts that went along with it: *"Who are you to talk about living boldly? See there, you're not meant to do this. It's too hard. No one will take you seriously."*

If it hadn't been for several authors being open with me and sharing their own challenges while writing, I may have either still been writing this book, or may have put it on the shelf unfinished.

The point is, sometimes there is never a right time to do something, and sometimes you just have to push through even when things around you seem contrary to what you are doing.

I also started taking my own advice, to have more fun and enjoy my journey even on the days I could hardly get out of bed or concentrate and make sense out of my own writing.

I began to truly see the importance of having a team and hired someone to help me finish my story. While the whole process of writing was not fun, it was a wildly growing experience and I am grateful for it.

During this writing time, my "BOLD" looked different depending on the situation. At times it was letting my brain heal and do nothing, which was the hardest because I despise being still. Other times it was sharing about my book with people, which was way out of my comfort zone because I would much rather listen than talk. And other times it was learning to say "no" and letting go of commitments that were impeding on other priorities. And then at times I had to think differently and not get caught up in my own drama with my health. I had to keep trusting in God's promises that He would give me strength; after all, I feel this book was His idea.

So whatever journey you endeavor on, know that each one will look different and require you to be bold on different levels. Embrace it. My dream for you is to unleash your 'inner bold' and have the time of your life while doing it!

— Barbara Gustavson
November 23, 2018

Acknowledgments

First and foremost, I would like to thank my husband, Paul, and my children, Michael and Ryan, for always believing in me and encouraging me to be the best I can be. You brought laughter into my life and it has been a wonderful adventure with you in it.

To my writing coaches, Chris Jones and Stephanie Wetzel, and editors Maude Campbell and Amy Metheny, who helped me organize my thoughts and strengthen my communication throughout the writing process: Thank you for believing in my message.

To Paul Martinelli, Melanie Yost, Sylvia Frejd, and John Maxwell: Thank you for believing in me!

To my JMT Family: You have been that family community I have longed for my whole life. It would take forever to list everyone, so thank you ALL.

To my encouragers: Throughout this process, you have helped guide me to find my strengths. A special thank you to Patti Hanrath, Trudy Menke, Christina Carson, Alayna Stiffler, Mike Harbour, Christy Escher, Cynthia Armbrister, Sheri Griffin, and Bob and Nancy Kittridge.

To those I interviewed: Your transparency helped me focus on what was most needed for my readers.

To those who allowed me to share their personal story: Dawn, Paige, Denise, Karen, Andi, Paul, Nick, Stacy, and lastly mom (I know you would approve, thank you for your vulnerability and sharing your personal journey with me.

To my book launch team: Thank you for wisdom and support to make this message stronger.

To my sister: Thank you for encouraging me to make my mark in the world.

To Dad: Thank you for making me get back in the saddle. It was truly one of the greatest gifts and lessons you imparted to me.

To Mom: Even though you aren't physically here, you are here with me every day. Thank you for always believing me and encouraging me to be myself. I miss you with all my heart.

To God: Thank you for making me just like I am and never giving up on me.

Finally, to all you readers: Thank you for betting on YOU and desiring to live more boldly. You are packed full of potential and I hope this book helps you explore the greatness that is already inside you. I would love to hear from you. Find me on Twitter, or on my website. Let me know how this book has encouraged you to find your 'inner bold'!

— Barbara Gustavson

http://www.barbaragustavson.com

Notes

Chapter 1

1. *The "Parable of the Talents"* Matthew 25:14–30

Chapter 2

1. The concept of Bogus Story, came from my mentor Melissa West, *Xtreme Results*, www.xrcoaching.com

2. *Love Does: Discover a Secretly Incredible Life in an Ordinary World* by Bob Goff

Chapter 3

1. *Change Your Brain, Change Your Life (Revised and Expanded): The Breakthrough Program for Conquering Anxiety, Depression, Obsessiveness, Lack of Focus, Anger, and Memory Problems* by Dr. Daniel Amen

2. *Your Survival Instinct Is Killing You: Retrain Your Brain to Conquer Fear and Build Resilience* by Marc Schoen and Kristin Loberg

3. *Are You a Fraud?* by Melanie Yost, http://www.discovernextstep.com/are-you-a-fraud/

4. *The Deeper Path: Five Steps That Let Your Hurts lead to Your Healing* by Kary Oberbrunner

5. *Start with Why: How Great Leaders Inspire Everyone to Take Action* by Simon Sinek

6. *Find Your Why: A Practical Guide for Discovering Purpose for You and Your Team* by Simon Sinek

Chapter 4

1. Nick Vujicic, www.attitudeisaltitude.com

2. *The Soul of Money: Transforming Your Relationship with Money and Life* by Lynne Twist

3. *Good Timber* a poem by Douglas Malloch

4. *Role of Wind in a Trees Life* by Anupum Pant, http://awesci.com/the-role-of-wind-in-a-trees-life/

5. *Biosphere 2* at University of Arizona http://biosphere2.org

Chapter 5

1. Naomi Watts interview *Tall Poppy Syndrome*, https://people.com/movies/naomi-watts-explains-australias-tall-poppy-syndrome-and-how-she-dealt-with-it/

2. *A Return to Love: Reflections on the Principles of "A Course in Miracles"* by Marianne Williamson

Chapter 6

1. *Safe People: How to Find Relationships that are Good for You and Avoid Those That Aren't* by Dr. Henry Cloud and John Townsend

2. *Resilience: Facing Down Rejection and Criticism on the Road to Success,* by Mark McGuinness

3. *The "Parable of the Wineskins"* Luke 5:27-39

4. *The 15 Invaluable Laws of Growth: Live Them and Reach Your Potential* by John C. Maxwell

Chapter 7

1. *Braving the Wilderness: The Quest for True Belonging and the Courage to Stand Alone* by Brené Brown

2. Harvard Business Review, *Resilience is About How you Endure*, https://hbr.org/2016/06/resilience-is-about-how-you-recharge-not-how-you-endure

3. *Micro-Resilience: Minor Shifts for Major Boosts in Focus, Drive, and Energy* by Bonnie St. John

Chapter 8

1. *Tony Robins,* www.tonyrobins.com

2. *Boundaries for Leaders: Results, Relationships, and Being Ridiculously in Charge* by Dr. Henry Cloud

3. *Is Gratitude Good For You? The evidence on giving thanks,* by Alex Wood, Jeffrey Froh, and Adam Geraghty, https://www.psychologytoday.com/us/blog/evidence-based-living/201611/is-gratitude-good-you-0

4. *How Being Grateful Year Round Can Impact Your Mood,* https://www.amenclinics.com/blog/grateful-year-round-can-impact-mood/

Chapter 9

1. *Facts on People with Aphasia,* https://www.aphasia.org/

2. *Virtual World Society,* http://virtualworldsociety.org/

3. *Seasons of Life,* by Jim Rohn

Chapter 10

1. *Intentional Living: Choosing a Life that Matters* by John C. Maxwell

About the Author

Barbara Gustavson, Founder of *Discover Next Step*, equips purpose-driven people to know their value, live boldly, and contribute their gifts to the world. She encourages them to embrace their strengths and imperfections, make peace with their past, and live fully with no apologies.

Barbara followed her own calling to live her life with meaning and provide a deeper level of service to others. To learn more about Barbara, visit her website or social media.

- www.DiscoverNextStep.com
- www.linkedin.com/in/barbaragustavson
- www.twitter.com/BVGustavson

•••

Want to take steps in living more boldly and receive encouragement to help you reach your goals no matter what season you're in? Go to www.innerbold.com and ask to join the FB community!

UNLEASH YOUR INNER BOLD

Imagine being led through a transformational process where you gain the clarity you need and develop a customized, doable plan for your next steps in your life and business.

One-on-one Coaching Program
On-line Experience

Full Weekend Intensive for Women
Individual and Small Group
On-site Experience

Find Out More Today

UNLEASH YOUR INNER BOLD

Bring Barbara Into Your Business or Organization

SPEAKER. FACILITATOR. AUTHOR. COACH.

Barbara understands the importance of BOLD leadership. She believes that truly genuine leadership can't exist without the *want* and *willingness* to be bold enough to first lead yourself.

Through her authentic approach, she helps individuals and teams uncover their strengths, clarify their vision, and breakthrough on strategies that will impact their world.

Contact Barbara today to begin the conversation!

---

www.DiscoverNextStep.com

Made in USA - Crawfordsville, IN
88157_9780997687224
02.12.2021 1906